Dresses

TIME-SAVING SEWING WITH A CREATIVE TOUCH

weekend sewer's guide to

Dresses

TIME-SAVING SEWING WITH A CREATIVE TOUCH

Kate Mathews

LARK
BOOKS

Dedication

To all lovers of fabric and sewing.

Art Director: Dana Irwin

Photography: Richard Babb

Illustrations: Pete Adams, Lisa Mandle, Jennifer Swofford, Bernadette Wolf

Production: Bobby Gold, Dana Irwin

Library of Congress Cataloging-in Publication Data

Mathews, Kate.

   The weekend sewer's guide to dresses : time-saving sewing
with a creative touch / by Kate Mathews. -- 1st ed.

     p.   cm.

   "A Lark sewing book."

   Includes index.

   ISBN 1-57990-015-1

   1. Dressmaking. 2.Machine sewing. I. Title.

TT515.M285   1998   97-18402

646.4'32--dc21   CIP

10 9 8 7 6 5 4 3 2 1

First Edition

Published by Lark Books

50 College St.

Asheville, NC 28801, US

© 1998, Lark Books

Distributed by Random House, Inc., in the United States, Canada, the United Kingdom,
   Europe, and Asia

Distributed in Australia by Capricorn Link (Australia) Pty Ltd., P.O. Box 6651, Baulkham
   Hills Business Centre, NSW 2153, Australia

Distributed in New Zealand by Tandem Press Ltd., 2 Rugby Rd., Birkenhead, Auckland,
   New Zealand

Printed in the United States

CONTENTS

We spend our lives in a succession of dresses, and our personal histories are often marked by dress milestones—Sunday school dress, recital dress, ballet dress, prom dress, wedding dress, maternity dress, cocktail dress, little black dress, mother of the bride dress, evening dress. We remember every one of them in intimate detail and exactly how they looked in the mirror. We remember if we felt fabulous in them or if they never looked quite right, how they swirled when we danced and how they made us feel beautiful and confident. We remember some with extra special fondness, because they are associated with special events or favorite times in our lives. Others we hate for no good reason other than the fact we wore them at sad or embarrassing times, and we dread that they somehow might end up in our closets again. But the fact that we remember them at all illustrates just how important the dress is to a personal sense of style throughout life.

THE DRESS— PILLAR OF FASHION, CORNERSTONE OF A WARDROBE

Fashion trends and seasons are built on the dress, never on the skirt or blouse. We hear about the return of the chemise or the little black dress, the "rediscovery" of the empire waist style, or the renewed popularity of the mini dress. Trends in dress design seem to come around like celestial comets— thrilling new sights that we swear we've seen before. They may even be still hanging in our closets from the last time they were in style. We can't bear to get rid of them, so we wait patiently until the next time they are "in" because everyone knows that if you wait long enough, all styles will come around again. On the other hand, we may have given up fashion long ago. We don't care what they say in the style capitals of the world. Our tastes are set, our styles consistent from year to year.

Considering the importance of the dress in our lives and our closets, it's odd that many women say they don't sew dresses. Instead, they report a preference for interchangeable ensembles of skirts and tops. A mix-and-match approach to wardrobe planning may be sensible for day-to-day wear, but when a special event is on the horizon, the perfect choice is most often a dress. Or when we're running late in the morning and don't have time to put together an outfit of separates, a dress is a quick and easy way to look well put together.

A dress is so versatile and can serve so many functions perfectly, whether it's a conservative princess seam coat dress for a business meeting, a flirty little wrap dress for a once-a-year party, or a loose and comfortable tent dress for doing the weekly shopping. They can be elegant, casual, feminine, or businesslike; dressed up or down with coordinating accessories, or perfect by themselves in classic simplicity.

When we sewers find a good dress, we don't care what the designers or fashion magazines say—we just keep making it up again and again. The princess seams may be flattering, the cut of the skirt hangs just right, or the simple lines are easy to alter and quick to sew. Whatever the reason, it's a favorite and we keep coming back to it. The pattern tissue gets old and fragile, barely holding together for all the pin holes, and we have to retrace it onto a sturdier paper before it finally falls apart. The instructions get marked up with notes

about changes we made to improve the fit or include a favorite shortcut. The construction steps become so familiar that we can make the dress without referring to them, or we take off in our own directions and invent new assembly steps

as we go. Each time we pull the pattern out of the envelope, we think back to all the versions we've made before and wonder: How can I make it different this time? What special touch can I add to turn this old favorite into a fresh, new look? Or how can I simplify it, without sacrificing its special quality, so I can get it done by Saturday's dinner party?

This book can help in two ways—by giving you ideas for adding new flair to a classic dress pattern and sharing tips for making it up quickly. Everything you need is here, from hints for inspiring creativity to ideas for unusual accessories and special finishing touches.

GETTING THE CREATIVE JUICES FLOWING

Designer workbook pages will show you how easy it can be to put ideas together for fresh, new design options and combine them with fabrics and trim—so you can make the same dress in lots of different ways for several different looks. You will also see what other sewers have done to add their personal design signatures to standard styles, including the tent dress, shirtwaist, princess style, sheath, and coat dress. The abundant creativity evident in these dresses will surely spark some good ideas for adding your own unique style signature to your next sewing project.

BARBARA MORGAN

GET READY

GET SET...

When you study your favorite dress pattern and dream up ways to make a completely new version, you don't want to spend months doing it. That's why we've combined tips for efficient and time-saving sewing with suggestions for adding creative flair. You'll find pointers for planning your time, along with weekly plans for each of the garments that tell you how the designer made the most of weekday evenings, leaving her time to assemble and complete the dress on the weekend (hence the title of this book). You'll also find tips for organizing your sewing area, selecting styles and fabrics, and using available tools and equipment to help you get the most out of the limited time you have to sew. Technical help—from fitting, stitching, and assembly tips to finishing touches and correcting errors—will guide you effortlessly through the process of renewing an old standby dress style and enhancing it with your individual stamp of creativity. Before long, your own dress creations will be the new milestones of a memorable wardrobe.

SEW!

GET READY:
Techniques for time-saving sewing

You may have heard the saying, "If you want to get something done, ask a busy woman." There's a lot of truth to this. Women's lives are jam-packed with activities and responsibilities, yet somehow they seem to get everything done: attending meetings, keeping appointments, managing a home, picking up and dropping off everything from children at soccer practice to clothes at the dry cleaners. Day-planning schedule books get crammed with notes, reminders get tacked up on the refrigerator, and brains fill to overflowing with important items to remember.

Then, after a full day of work or running around, evenings are claimed by cooking, gardening, chores, meetings, and all manner of entertainment options. Newspapers entice you with great-sounding events, interesting books pile up that you want to read, and new organizations that appeal to your varied interests—gardening, upholstery classes, stock market investment clubs, French classes, and more—invite your membership.

Somehow, in the midst of this flurry of activity, you still manage to keep up with the new sewing patterns and fabrics that come out every season. But getting any actual sewing done these days is more and more challenging. Despite all the time-saving conveniences of modern life, schedules seem busier than ever. The advertisements for computers, fax machines, answering machines, and electronic appliances all promise a more streamlined and productive life that will increase or enhance your leisure time. Sure, they all help you be more productive, but the more you get done, the longer your "To Do" list gets. There seems to be less free time, rather than more.

You dream about taking a week's vacation with nothing but your sewing machine, enjoying entire days of stitching, and visualizing a whole wardrobe of wonderful new garments to wear home on the last day. But you know it's just a dream, so you downsize your fantasies to the weekend coming up—two whole days relatively free of commitment or obligation. You just might be able to sew up a new dress for next week's reception, if only Saturday and Sunday don't get derailed with last-minute work deadlines or a family crisis.

How are you ever going to find more time to sew, when your favorite activity always seems to get bumped to the bottom of the list? After a long day, you're either too busy or too tired to sit down at the sewing machine, so you fall exhausted into bed and dream about sewing all weekend long. But don't deceive yourself—if you wait to sew until you have big parcels of unscheduled time, you'll never get anything done.

The better alternative is to take control of your schedule, plan your time, and organize sewing into manageable, flexible tasks that you can fit into your very busy everyday life. It takes a focused commitment, but that's the easy part for any sewer who has a passion for working with cloth. What is more difficult is the "how-to" of controlling your time. For some helpful tips, read on.

A Stitch in Time

Search out the empty nooks and crannies of time in your daily schedule and use them to make progress on a current project. For example, do your handsewing while waiting for the dentist or baste a seam while waiting for water to boil. You can get something done in as little as two minutes!

Planning your sewing time

The first step in maximizing time for your favorite activity is to look at sewing with the same critical eye you use in any other time management exercise. Just as any other important task or commitment, you've got to give sewing the priority it deserves and fit it into your schedule. If you manage to exercise three days a week, get your hair done once a week, or put dinner on the table every night, you can manage to sew regularly every week. Whether sewing is your personal form of therapy, a creative outlet, or a money-saving wardrobe maker, you deserve to make time for it.

PRIORITIZE

If you want to find more time to sew, you've got to rank sewing right up there with medical appointments, regular meetings, and volunteer obligations. It's just as important as

any, and maybe all, of the other obligations that stake claims on your time. Like most women, you probably put your own interests aside to get other things done or take care of other people—children, parents, spouses, friends, lovers, pets.

It must be genetic, but women just don't take the time for themselves that they should. This is surprising because women are also very adept at doing several things at once,

juggling many different commitments. However, women don't see to it that sewing is one of the activities being juggled—they set it aside as "less important" and dream of long, uncommitted days that never really happen. Work, home, and family always come first. Any time that's left over gets eaten up by television, telephones, laundry, and the other details of everyday life. Well, it's time to let the dishes and laundry sit, just for one hour, so you can sit down and sew a couple of seams or plan the next outfit on your list. Make it a priority!

A Stitch in Time

Enter sewing time into your daily schedule or day-planning book just like any other time commitment, such as meetings, appointments, or exercise.

SCHEDULE

Sewing deserves an entry on your calendar or a reminder note on your refrigerator, just like the dentist's appointment card and the parent-teacher conference notice. Open up your day-planning book or buy one of the time management books available at any office supply store, and block out sewing time as you would any other commitment. Start slotting a bit of time on one or two days a week, and gradually expand until you are working it in every day! Schedule 15 minutes before breakfast, 30 minutes after work, or one hour after dinner. It doesn't matter how much time you schedule or when, just block it in so the time doesn't get preempted by something else. If you don't want the words, "Sewing Time," to be right out there in black and white, where everyone can see them, call it "Production Time," or "Brainstorming," or "Studio Hour," or anything. Whatever you call it, when you see it on your schedule regularly, you'll learn to automatically stop or disengage what you're doing and move on to sewing. Unless a crisis takes precedence, you'll have no excuse for avoiding the sewing machine—it's right there on your schedule for the next 30 minutes or one hour.

DIVERSIFY

Another secret to maximizing your sewing productivity is to look at sewing as many different functions instead of a single activity. Each of those different functions requires a different amount of time and type of concentration or attention. Shopping for patterns and fabrics, scoping out styles in the department stores, selecting buttons and trims—these are all different "types" of sewing time than the hours you spend at the machine or cutting table. Once you break up sewing into various components, it's easier to coordinate a specific function with the amount of time available, amount of energy you have, and what other activities may be going on at the same time—dinner, for example.

Some of these function categories include collecting ideas, selecting patterns, fabric shopping, prewashing and fabric preparation, pattern evaluation and alteration, fitting, cutting, marking, interfacing, assembly, pressing, finishing, accessorizing. There are probably many more, but you get the idea—break up the enormous territory of sewing into manageable, do-able tasks that require concrete amounts of time.

Then diversify your scheduling entries to match the activity. "Sewing" is too broad a category to take seriously when you've only got a lunch hour or

a few minutes. Break it down into smaller chunks, and all of a sudden a lunch hour can help you make progress on a project. For example, use your lunch hour to cruise the mall looking for inspiration or stake out 30 minutes after work to stop in at the store and select some buttons to finish a project. You'll also find that if you vary the function you're trying to schedule, it will be easier to get it in your date book, get it done, and mark it off your "To Do" list.

MAKE THE MOST OF AVAILABLE TIME

There are several old sayings about not wasting time, and it may be helpful to dredge up some of them, make them into little posters, and pin them up in a visible place. You will continually remind yourself to be as productive as possible with the little bits of time you have. The secret is to look for the empty nooks and crannies of time in your schedule, just as you search out the little bits of extra space in your house for storage. Where are the brief segments that get wasted, the fragments of time that escape unnoticed or unused?

Find them, mark them, look at them as opportunities...and then use them! Press a seam while you're waiting for the water to boil. Baste a seam while you're waiting for the iron to warm up. Cut out patterns while watching television or talking on the phone (that may be why they invented speaker phones!). Bring hemming or other handwork to the doctor's office, to finish while you wait—why waste time looking at magazines? If you forgot to bring handwork, then use the time to scan the magazines for inspiration or fashion ideas.

A Stitch in Time

Keep a measuring tape or short ruler in your purse, for measuring fashion details and features of ready-to-wear and also for measuring yourself when you're trying on clothes or considering sewing patterns.

get what you need. If you come upon some dreamy fabric that you can't live without, and the bolt is almost gone, you'll be able to check your list of patterns, pick the right one for this heart-stopping fabric, and buy the correct amount. There's no chance you'll get it home, discover that you're a little short, only to return to the store the next day and find the fabric sold out. When you are prepared, you'll prevent "heart-stopping" from turning into "heart-breaking."

A Stitch in Time

Assess your garment needs before you head to the fabric store or mall. It's easier to make smart choices when you know what wardrobe gaps you have to fill.

Carry a small notepad or sketch book with you at all times. You can sketch an idea or a wonderful detail you've spotted on someone walking by. Jot down ideas or tips you've overheard right on the spot, instead of trying to remember them later. When someone gives you the name of a contact, title of a book to read, or great idea—write it down. You never know when it might come in handy. And once it's written down, you can free up the brain cells in your memory and put them to work on more interesting projects.

Double up your errand time. For instance, slip into the fabric store with your list of interfacing needs after you're finished with the grocery shopping, or look for accessories for that new dress while you're shopping for a family gift. Maximize your chore time. For example, prewash fabric in between loads of family clothing, or take out five minutes to clean and oil your machine while you're vacuuming the sewing area.

BE PREPARED

That sounds like a Girl Scout slogan, but it really does work! Make and carry lists with you at all times—lists of yardages for favorite patterns, pattern numbers you want to check out, notions you need to pick up. When you happen to have 20 extra minutes, you can dart into the store and

If you're shopping for patterns or accessories, carry swatches of the fabrics you already own to help you make a perfect match. Make up a little plastic bag or a notebook of your swatches, marked with the amount of yardage you already have or need to buy. When you find the right pattern, you won't have to wait until you get home to see if you have enough fabric. When shopping for coordinated accessories, you probably won't be able to visualize exactly how they will go with garments at home unless you've got swatches with you. You may run the risk of buying a brand new pair of shoes to match a dress you just finished sewing, only to find that your memory of the dress color was way off. To prevent this frustrating and inconvenient scenario, save a few scraps from that dress to carry with you when you're looking for the perfect shoes or a coordinating belt, scarf, or vest. It will take much less time to find accessories, and you will end up with a wardrobe of pieces that coordinate flawlessly.

Another way to be prepared is to carry a tape measure and use it to check yardage widths or features of ready-to-wear

you might want to duplicate. Or tuck away some favorite buttons that are waiting for the perfect mate—they may inspire you to consider a piece of fabric you would not have noticed otherwise. Get the idea? Carry whatever you need to take advantage of an opportunity when it presents itself. Planning your time is a skill like any other. You get better at it the more you do it. And you may discover pretty quickly that you're actually getting more sewing done. Isn't that what it's all about?

15 THINGS YOU CAN DO *in 15 minutes*

When you've only got 15 minutes available, don't let it waste away. Use those precious minutes to get something done, whether it's planning, marking, stitching, or pressing. Working in 15-minute chunks of time can be a lot more gratifying than waiting for a free day or weekend. You'll eventually finish the garment, but you might wait forever for that free day. In 15 minutes, you can complete any of these tasks:

1. Review a pattern to determine fabric needs and construction details.

2. Play around with fabric swatches to come up with new garment ideas.

3. Clean, oil, and rethread your sewing machine.

4. Mark notches and dots on a cut-out pattern.

5. Try on a muslin sample and check the fit.

6. Fuse interfacing to several garment pieces.

7. Pin and stitch a couple of darts.

8. Sew several straight seams.

9. Finish side seams on the serger.

10. Ease and baste a set-in sleeve into the armhole.

11. Stitch, clip, turn, and press a cuff.

12. Pin up a hem.

13. Blind-stitch part of a hem.

14. Do a final pressing of a new garment.

15. Clean up one project and get ready for the next one.

Developing creative ideas

Is this scenario familiar to you? You pull out your favorite dress pattern and look forward to sewing it up again—it fits perfectly, looks great, and goes together effortlessly. You've made this style many times before, and you have been happy with the results every time. While studying the drawing on the pattern envelope, you wonder, "What can I do to make it different this time? Surely there's something I can add or change to make this look special. I've got to think of some new creative touch—where do I start?"

A Stitch in Time

Carry a little notebook with you at all times, so you can jot down or sketch ideas when they come to you or when you notice an interesting fashion detail on someone walking by.

Finding time to come up with creative ideas is even harder than finding time to sew. But it can be done the same way—by taking advantage of opportunities that arise and making the most of the time you have. First off, don't be scared by the pressure to be creative. A creative touch is often just a simple embellishment or new twist. In fact, simplicity is usually surprisingly innovative. It's the fresh treatment, the unexpected detail that makes something unique. After years of successful sewing experience, you probably already know more about inspiration and creativity than you think you do—so take heart.

Keep your eyes open

The secret to finding inspiration is sharpening your powers of observation and learning to consider alternatives—some people call it "thinking outside the box." It involves breaking out of your customary thought patterns and venturing into new territory. Everywhere you go and everything you see has the potential to serve up an idea you can put to good use. All you have to do is notice, and remember. That's why it's so important to carry a notebook, so that no good idea gets by you before jotting it down or sketching it roughly.

Don't worry about your drawing skills; the important thing is to record what you noticed—you're the only one who will see it.

Observe people, everywhere—at work, the mall, church, the airport. Study their clothes and their sense of style. Keep an eye out for interesting color combinations, unusual applications of trim, simple variations on classic styles, innovative accessorizing, anything that makes you stop and say, "Wow, that's a great idea." File it away for future reference, and you'll be amazed at how many times an idea will come back to you, to be altered just a little bit or combined with something else to result in a fabulous new look.

This is what the famous designers do—they study the world around them, looking for something they can reinterpret for their new collections. One season, they "notice" military garments, and you see epaulets and brass buttons on everything coming down the runway. Another season, they "rediscover" lace and all the models are wearing frilly, lacy confections. Of course, the designers have big travel budgets that allow them to go to Barbados or China for their field work. But you can do the same thing on Main Street or at the mall. Just keep your eyes open and take notes.

Monitor the fashion and style worlds

Spend a lunch hour or two at the library, leafing through the current fashion and sewing magazines. You'll see what those famous designers scoped out during their travels, as well as plenty of other in-fashion styles. The clothes in the magazine pages are usually too outrageous for real life, but they almost always feature some details you can adapt. If it's

A Stitch in Time

Think of the whole world around you as an inspiration laboratory. Keep your eyes open, and you'll be surprised how often and in how many places you'll notice good ideas that you can use.

important to you to have a current wardrobe of in-fashion styles, regular scanning of the magazines is a great way to see what's happening elsewhere, before it gets to your home town. Check out the advertisements, too; they can be a wealth of ideas for accessorizing and other details.

Your favorite sewing shop will probably become a regular stop on your inspiration tour. Staff members of most stores try to make up new patterns soon after they come out so you can look, touch, and think about how they'll work for you. Take a few moments to chat with the owner or sales help. If they have been to a recent home sewing or fabric show, they can share what's coming up in the way of new styles, materials, and decorative effects.

Make a trip to the mall and breeze through the department stores to see what ready-to-wear styles and colors are "in" each season. This is an easy way to keep up with the fashion world and allows you to actually get your hands on the fabrics and take a close look at construction details. Whip out your measuring tape to check the season's hem length, or try clothes on to see which of the new styles flatter you most. If your favorite department store is far away, make a field trip with some sewing friends or request a mail order catalog (if available) to see what's hanging on the racks.

Television is a good source for ideas, too. Check your local schedule for regular programs on fashion and style; they often feature the latest and newest from everywhere. You're bound to see something you like, and you can work it into your own sewing. But don't stop at the fashion shows. Watch the home decorating shows, too, and look for crossover ideas you can adapt to garment sewing. You might see drapery fabrics that would be perfect for garments (if Scarlett O'Hara can use curtain fabric for a great dress, you can too!). Upholstery braids

and tassels can lend a military look to jackets, and piped seams can add flair to a double-breasted coat pattern.

The "home dec" shows and magazines are also great resources for advance notice about color trends. The newest paint colors will likely turn up sooner or later in the fabric stores, and interior design techniques such as marbling or sponge painting can often be simulated in cloth. If they work beautifully on the sofa or the wall, why not put the same ideas to work in your sewing room?

CREATE YOUR OWN INSPIRATION LIBRARY

Start clipping, snipping, and collecting ideas. Surround yourself with visual stimulation and inspiring images. Pin up your own sketches or fill a bulletin board with photos clipped from magazines. Keep the clippings out where you can see them, and sooner or later (probably sooner) your own creativity will be sparked—and, eureka, you'll discover just the right touch for that favorite pattern.

If you don't have room for a bulletin board or permanent display wall, make up a scrapbook or sketchbook. Tape or paste photos and sketches inside, and attach snippets of lace or trim that seem to pair themselves well with the images. Make notes about how you would alter or adapt the idea, or what changes you would make to put your own imprint on it.

Alternatively, keep file folders for different idea categories—home interiors, jackets, dresses, accessories, etc. Put your clippings in the files, and when you're getting ready to start a new project, go through the files looking for ideas that might be useful. Some of your clippings might seem a bit far-fetched, but no matter. There are plenty of ideas buried there for innovative color combinations, fabric treatments, and special effects. Did you see a neat diagonal stripe effect in an upholstery ad? Duplicate it along the hem of a skirt. An interesting tucked bodice in a wedding gown? Adapt it to the front panels of a vest. A great tooled leather handbag at the store? Try the same effect in an appliquéd Ultrasuede coat.

Change the selection on your bulletin board or in your scrapbook periodically. You need to refresh your inspiration sources and create new opportunities for seeing something you didn't notice before. Rotate the selection by season or just when you need a different point of view. The designers do this every fashion season, so why not you?

A Stitch in Time

Start with a technique you want to try—appliqué, pleating, tucking, smocking, whatever. Build the idea for the garment from the technique, and select fabrics to accentuate technical effects.

START WITH THE FABRIC

Another great source of inspiration is your own fabric stash or local fabric store. Use fabric as the basic building block of great garments. Evaluate design elements in the fabric to identify starting points for creativity. For example, manipulate the fabric's stripes or checks to create special effects. Or work as a painter, composing color blocks with different solids. Solid-color fabric can also be a canvas for decorative stitching effects, providing a great background for contrasting colors. Pastels, brights, solids, patterns—they all suggest different approaches.

Play with your swatches, putting them in different combinations, pinning them up where you can see them. If you belong to any of the mail order fabric clubs, you'll accumulate mounds of swatches over time. Use them like paint chips, to help you visualize different looks. Handling the swatches and feeling the texture, as well as looking at them, can often suggest appropriate styles and will get you excited about working with material.

In your mind's eye, put together outfits starting from your clippings, fabrics, buttons, or trims. Or start with a particular

technique you want to use—pleating, for example—and visualize a garment that makes the most of pleated fabric. Push yourself, think outside the box, dream up new possibilities—it gets easier the more you do it. Here, again, that old adage speaks the truth: "Practice makes perfect." Many of your ideas may be discarded, but they just might lead to the one great idea that you finally use. The fabulous finished garment will get lots of admiring compliments. Only you will know the creative process that went into it.

A Stitch in Time

Look around for inspiration, but trust yourself to come up with the best ideas—you will!

A Stitch in Time

Turn on your creative radar when you're out shopping at the mall, grocery store, antique row, or in the boutiques. You can pick up ideas from what others are wearing, what's hanging on the racks, or old treasures from the past. That's how the designers do it—you can, too.

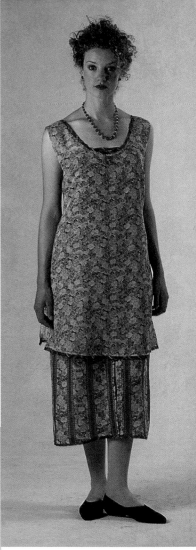

DESIGNER LISA MANDLE STARTS WITH THIS SIMPLE TANK DRESS WITH ATTACHED "APRON" FROM HER ONLY ONE COLLECTION AND THEN VARIES IT FIVE WAYS. THE DIFFERENT FABRIC COMBINATIONS AND CHANGING SELECTION OF BINDINGS, TRIMS, AND JEWELED OR BEADED DETAILS (ABOVE RIGHT) CREATE AN ENTIRE WARDROBE OF LOOKS FROM ONE BASIC STYLE.

A Stitch in Time

Keep it simple. The best ideas are often stripped down to the basics. The simplest touch can be the crowning glory of a garment. Overdo a special effect and it will disappear into a confusing mess.

A Stitch in Time

Don't be afraid to sketch your ideas. Nobody else but you has to see the drawings, and they might lead you in a new direction.

Selecting styles and patterns

If you have limited time for sewing, you don't want to use it up struggling with a complicated pattern or difficult fabric—it's too stressful. Save the laboratory experiments for your vacation, when you might have some extra hours to work through a new pattern or figure out how to tame a finicky fabric. But during your normal week, depend on what's predictable. The goal is to get more sewing accomplished—the method is to streamline and simplify the steps.

Start with the garment style. You probably already know which styles you prefer, which look best on you, and which are most comfortable to wear. In fact, if you study the pattern books and fashion magazines over the years, you'll see the same basic styles coming around again and again. The reason is because they look predictably good on the figures they're designed for. It's the details and enhancements that update them year to year, but the basic silhouette remains pretty much the same.

If you, too, follow the guideline of the basic flattering silhouette, using creative enhancements to change the look from year to year, you'll always look great and your garments will have enduring appeal. Plus, you'll save plenty of time in the long run. Why use precious hours to experiment with a totally new and untested style, when you want to finish a dress this weekend and you already know what looks good on you? Stick with what you know—you've already worked out the fitting requirements and construction details. You can then add special touches or make subtle changes to the basic underlying style "skeleton," as the designer did on the preceding pages.

RULES FOR FIGURE FLATTERY

By the time girls become women, they have internalized the basic rules of figure flattery. These lessons are taught in the pages of fashion magazines and sewing books, and reinforced in the fitting rooms of the world. You can see for yourself their naked truth in front of the mirror and, no matter how much you try to defy them, you "feel" their truth in clothes that flatter your figure, or don't.

For example, vertical lines lengthen the figure and make you appear taller, while horizontal lines broaden the figure and can add visual weight. If you're trying to add height and camouflage broad hips, you'll find that up-and-down stripes or vertical seam treatments will do the job. You won't be happy with the appearance of a side-to-side striped dress that has a hipline belt. The idea is to control the observing eye, moving it in the direction you want and away from the figure characteristics you'd just as soon remained invisible. Other basic rules of figure flattery that you will probably recognize from your own experience include:

■ light colors add weight; dark colors reduce weight.

■ cinched-in waist styles do not create the illusion

A Stitch in Time

If you want to detract attention from a very curvy figure, choose styles with straight lines or seams. Sleek architectural outfits and straight column dresses are good choices.

of a small waist on a large-waisted figure; the better choice is to select styles that draw attention away from the waistline altogether.

■ dropped-waist styles attract attention to the hip area and are not a good choice if you're trying to camouflage your hips.

■ a solid dark color, from neckline to hemline, is slimming, and even more so when worn with matching dark hose.

■ empire or raised waist styles enhance large busts.

If you're a little rusty on these lessons about figure flattery, your local library will have several handbooks on the subject. Once you review them, you may suddenly realize why a dress in your closet never looks good when you wear it. It might be because it draws attention to a part of your figure you wish was absent from your gene pool. By the way, this is a good time to remind you that your family genes have much more to do with figure type than any diet or exercise regimen. And, believe me, it's a lot more productive to learn how to enhance the positive aspects of your figure through knowledgeable style selection than it is to exact revenge on your ancestors for the tummy they bequeathed to you!

TESTING THE RULES

After you've reviewed the basic rules in the library books, it's time to conduct some primary research. Visit your local department store and spend some time in the fitting room with a selection of various styles. Or stay at home and try on everything in your closet. Go for variety, whether you like the individual garments or not. You aren't out to buy anything right now, just to review the truths about figure flattery. It doesn't matter if you hate the colors—ignore them and sim-

ply study the visual effect of the different styles.

Evaluate the appearance of general styles and construction types, to determine what looks best on your individual figure. This includes basic designs such as shirtwaist, fitted, or high-waisted, and construction details such as tailored, casual, or frilly. You will be amazed by how quickly the flatterers identify themselves and the detractors show their true colors. You'll probably also find them in perfect harmony with the rules described in the library books. But don't stop at general style and construction. Study the different necklines, sleeve lengths, hem lengths, color combinations—all the elements that contribute to the most flattering garments. Who knows, you might actually buy something. But the most important thing you'll take away is firsthand knowledge of what styles and details you should be reconstructing in your sewing room. You won't waste any more time on garments you won't wear.

SELECTING SEWING PATTERNS

With the fitting room results in mind, scan the pattern books looking for those basic styles that look great on your figure. It may be a sheath or no-waist chemise, a classic shirtwaist, distinguished double-breasted coat dress, or empire-waisted feminine frock. In every fashion season, just about every classic style makes an appearance—only the details make it different.

When you've identified the patterns that are right for your figure, look next for the time-saving features. These will probably be more visible in the line drawings than the photographs, so concentrate on the drawings; it's easy to miss something in a beautifully styled photo and end up with a garment that isn't quite right for you. Search for simple lines, uncomplicated seam treatments, and a minimum of finishing steps. In general, tailored styles will be more complex, with sharp corners that require precise and exacting stitches. Cuffed sleeves will require more assembly steps than straight sleeves. Shirt-style collars will take more time than shawl collars. The more segmented a garment, the more piecing, stitching, and pressing will be required.

Use your own experience as a touchstone. Think back to all the garments you've made and remember the steps that took more time or were more difficult. You already know from your own experience that a simple one-piece shift will go together in a snap, while an advanced designer dress can take weeks. So pick the patterns with the features that look best, and that take the least time or are easiest to assemble. If you hate setting in sleeves, look for dolman or raglan styles. If buttonholes are a nightmare for you, look for styles that don't require them—or devise easy ways to substitute other closures.

FOLLOW THE PATTERN COMPANIES' CLUES

The pattern companies themselves will often clue you in to the best styles for your figure and your schedule. Particular

styles may be recommended for certain figure types, such as rectangular, pear-shaped, or hourglass. Your personal experience may lead you to disagree, but these guidelines are often helpful for identifying flattering styles and construction details.

In addition, commercial patterns are often marked "Easy," or "Make it in an Hour," or "Intermediate." This identification system eases pattern selection for most sewers. However, your experience may lead you to believe that these labels can be deceptive. An "easy" pattern may omit certain construction steps you consider to be essential to good sewing. On the other hand, an "advanced" or "designer" pattern may be so detailed that step-by-step construction actually is quite logical and easy. Again, trust your own experience to guide you in selecting the patterns that will go together with a minimum of stress and confusion. This will save time in the long run, and will keep you in love with your sewing machine.

COORDINATING STYLES WITH FABRICS

Finally, when shopping for patterns, consider the fabrics you either love to work with or already have back home. Pull out your little baggie of swatches to review your fabric stash and feel them as you scan the pattern books. If you're shopping for pattern and fabric at the same time, get the pattern envelope first and carry it with you through the store as you handle the cloth.

Just as there are "rules" for figure enhancement, there are hard-earned truths about pairing pattern styles with fabric types. You've probably learned them firsthand when you tried to make a bias-cut dance dress out of a stiff seersucker—it just doesn't work! Stiff fabrics are poor choices for drapey, fluid styles, just as fluid fabrics are wrong for a crisp, well-defined look. It's better if you spend a little extra time at the outset, handling the fabric and imagining how it will look made up in the pattern you're holding. You won't run the risk of wasting time later on trying to figure out how to beat the fabric into submission, or finishing the garment only to never wear it.

IF YOU CAN'T FIND THE STYLE, IMPROVISE

If you've searched the pattern books and come up empty-handed, turn to your experience once again as a guide to improvising the perfect pattern. For example, you've got a favorite pattern at home, but it has an old-fashioned collar. You can redraw a new collar or shop for a new pattern with a great collar to put together with the old pattern at home. There is no law that says you have to make up sewing patterns exactly how the manufacturers recommend. You can use just the best pieces and put them in combination with the best pieces from other patterns, to create a custom "best" garment.

Choosing fabrics

The fabrics you choose are an important part of successfully finding more time to sew and ending up with more garments hanging in your closet. Luckily, there are many types of fabric available so it's not hard to find something luscious that is also easy to work with and care for. You want to search out the fabrics that don't require unusual treatment while sewing or unusual care after the garment is finished. Making sure your wardrobe is sewn from easy-care material keeps your clothes out of the dry cleaners, in your closet, and available to wear. This saves time and money!

When fabric shopping, examine the end of the bolt for the little tag or sticker that gives care instructions. If you don't find it, ask the salesperson for information about care requirements and allowances for shrinkage. If you do buy the fabric, make notes about how to care for it and attach to a swatch. Don't forget to include recommended pretreating or preshrinking tips. And don't forget to buy a little bit extra, if shrinkage is to be expected. Once the fabric joins your stash at home, it may be months until you match it up with a pattern and start working with it—by then, you might have forgotten how to handle it.

If care instructions cannot be found, listen to your inner voice of experience. If you've always had success pretreating and sewing with cottons, don't switch to linen when you're pressed for time on a project. Choose the fabrics you feel comfortable with, that you know how to sew with and care for. Experiment with challenging new high-tech cloth when you've got the time, or buy a small piece to sample—you might find that a new development in fabric, such as microfiber or fleece, can revolutionize your sewing productivity.

A Stitch in Time

Save time caring for your finished garments by sewing with low-maintenance fabrics, such as cottons and cotton knits, denim, corduroy, fleece, synthetic blends, machine-washable silks, microfiber, wool knits and crepes.

HOW WILL IT SEW?

In addition to easy care, look for easy-to-sew fabrics. There's no denying that some yardage is easier to work with. It behaves beautifully in the sewing machine, presses perfectly, and finishing seams is a breeze. Purchase the best quality fabric you can afford. It will sew easier and last longer than cheap material, which means you won't have to replace the garment for a longer time.

Some fabrics take more time and require more attention— velvet, metallics, chiffon, and slippery silks, among others. Save these for the specialty garments you're willing to spend the extra time on. When you've got limited time, choose the well-behaved cloth that seems to go together by itself.

Finally, try to select fabrics that coordinate well with your patterns and also enhance your figure. If you're trying to disguise too-generous curves, stay away from body-hugging styles made out of clingy knits. The pattern and fabric may be perfect together, but just aren't right for your figure.

TAKE THE GLOBAL VIEW

Before spending another hour shopping for fabric, take a bit of time and evaluate your wardrobe as a whole unit. You may look in your closet and see a bunch of separates or individual components, but try to get an overview of what's there. Is it mostly navy blue "dress for success" suits or small-print floral dresses? Do the components coordinate with each other, or do you have a closet full of "loners," pieces that go only with themselves? Mostly neutrals, pastels, or brights? Too many skirts and not enough tops? A glaring absence of special event dresses? What does the "whole" look like? If you know the answer, it's much easier to fill in the gaps and add new items that are just right.

This planning technique is a big time saver, not to mention a money saver. With a global view of what you have and what you need, you can concentrate your sewing time, energy, and budget on adding the most perfect companion garments to the cornerstone pieces. You don't waste time making one more piece that doesn't go with anything else in your closet, even though you love the fabric and it was on sale.

The global or overview strategy to building your wardrobe also saves shopping time. While you might enjoy strolling the aisles of your favorite fabric store, drooling over all the new arrivals, you know you're really there to find a particular piece that coordinates with a dress, suit, or ensemble you already have. When you're focused, you'll be more successful at getting what you need in the least amount of time. The result? You get back to your sewing machine quicker.

WHY DO YOU SEW?

An alternative to the overview strategy is to clearly define why exactly you sew and make your pattern and fabric purchases accordingly. If your sewing is purely for pleasure and personal therapy, you might choose to purchase ready-to-wear for your working wardrobe and spend your sewing time on creative art-to-wear garments or on that one special accent piece that will coordinate with the store-bought items. Or perhaps you get the most pleasure out of making things for your home, or for your children. If this is the case, don't waste your limited time agonizing over tailored slacks for yourself. Buy the pants, and use your time for sewing what you truly enjoy. If you sew to save money on a career wardrobe, check the pattern companies' special ensembles for mix-and-match options that can stretch a limited budget a long way, especially when put together with a few well-chosen accessories.

Once you understand the driving force behind your favorite activity, you'll know exactly which fabrics to be spending money on—fashion, specialty, bridal, drapery, or quilting. Just as your clothing should fit your lifestyle, your fabric selection should fit your sewing style. You'll save money, save time, and be happier with the results.

t's a simple truth that the more organized your sewing area is, the easier it is to sit down when you've got some free time and stitch a while. You probably live by this truth in the office, where an organized desk means you don't waste time looking for files, and in the kitchen, where meals go together faster and more efficiently when you've got what you need and you know where everything is. The sewing area isn't any different. You save time if needed supplies are on hand and stored where you can find them quickly. This is the goal, regardless of available square footage: a well-equipped area with essential supplies on hand.

Some women are lucky enough to have an entire room devoted to their favorite activity, while others have to carve out room for sewing in other areas of the home. Whether or not you've got the luxury of a sewing studio, being organized will save you time and money. If you can leave your sewing area set up as much as possible and ready to go whenever you've got a spare moment or two, you will

accomplish more. And, wherever your sewing area is, if you can post your inspiration board or keep your idea files close by, you'll be amazed at how your creativity will be stimulated when you can look up and see the great ideas you've been accumulating.

PLAN THE SPACE

Remember how you divided up sewing into different functions that can be completed in manageable fragments of time? Use the same strategy when planning your sewing area—divide up sewing into different activities that can take place in different areas. For example, cutting and marking are not an ongoing sewing activity, so they can be done periodically on the dining room table, a folding cutting board on the floor, or a double bed. Consider purchasing a roll-away folding cutting table that can double as a sideboard or buffet table when you don't need it for sewing. These tables usually fold down to a nice, small size that can easily be stowed in a narrow closet, behind the couch, or in a hallway under a painting. Some models feature convenient built-in storage drawers for scissors, measuring tape, and other cutting and marking supplies. Cutting tables are nice to have, but remember that you don't always need a large surface—just look for handy areas of your home that can be put to use. Smaller garment pieces can be cut and marked on the kitchen counter, coffee table, laundry table, or office desk.

Once the cutting and marking are completed, it's time to move to the sewing area—this is the focal point of your

A Stitch in Time

Think about mounting your various supply storage cabinets or boxes on casters, for easy rolling out when you're ready to work and back into a corner or closet when you're through.

space planning. If you've got the luxury of a whole room or section of a room, such as the laundry room or guest bedroom, count your blessings and set up the sewing machine and ironing board first. Everything else can be stowed elsewhere, but try to keep the sewing and pressing functions together and as set up as possible. In fact, a sewing friend's goal in life has been to leave the ironing board set up all the time. Some sewers like to have the ironing board right next to the sewing machine, and lowered to a seated level, so they can stitch a seam and then just swivel around to do the pressing, without getting up. Others like to keep the ironing board at a higher level and nearby, but not adjacent to the machine, so they can use ironing time as an opportunity to get up and stretch.

If you are still too strapped for space to leave anything permanently set up, call in your favorite handy-person to have a look at designing and building sewing stations in your home's hidden nooks and crannies—in a closet, under the stairway, off the kitchen, wherever your home yields up that extra space you previously thought was impossible to use. A little bit of ingenuity and some basic woodworking skills can do amazing things with drop-down ironing boards, sliding shelves, roll-away tables, and other space-saving miracles.

If you can't or don't want to build anything permanent, consider designing activity stations on casters, such as a small rolling table for the machine and one or two rolling shelf units or stacking basket units on casters. Then just roll them wherever you need them. Or use your creative talents to make a freestanding three-panel screen that can be put up when you want to conceal your sewing area. The screen panels can be plain canvas, silk-screened fabric, translucent paper, or knotted string lashed or stapled to a simple hinged wooden frame. You'll find that such a simple, functional camouflage trick can also double as an interior decorating bonus, attractively creating the impression of multiple spaces in your home.

EQUIP THE SPACE

Regardless of the amount of sewing space you have, it's essential to keep the supplies you need on hand. There's nothing more frustrating than getting fired up to start a new pattern after dinner, only to find that you're short on interfacing and forgot to buy the pocket lining. Here's where your lists come in handy, to help you keep your selection of supplies current and complete. Like a grocery list, this is basic

inventory control that keeps the shelves stocked with everything you need to sew.

Keep index cards or scrap paper right by the sewing machine or in your supply box. As you cut, mark, sew, press, or finish up a project, jot down the supplies you notice are getting low. If, after cutting out a new pattern, you've got just a scrap left of a favorite interfacing, jot it down so you'll know to buy some more before cranking up the next project. If you start the last spool of basic black serger thread, add it to the shopping list so you can buy more before the last one is used up. This is a simple, manual version of the sophisticated inventory control cash registers in your local grocery store—these high-tech machines deduct every purchased item from the inventory as the item leaves the store. If this item-by-item method keeps food on their shelves, it can keep thread in your bobbins.

Another supply-tracking method is to make a monthly or quarterly inventory sweep through your sewing area, instead of keeping up with things project by project as you use them. Survey everything you typically use—patterns, cutting

A Stitch in Time

Arrange your space according to your usual cleanliness habits; don't force yourself to be something you're not. If you're a slob, throw the thread ends and scraps on the floor, then clean them up later. If you're a neatnik, keep a small wastebasket close by or tape a paper lunch sack to the edge of your sewing table for trash.

and marking supplies, interfacing, lining, thread, etc.—and make a master list of items you're out of or getting low on. Then, schedule a lunchtime trip to the store to stock up.

No matter what method you use, keeping supplies on hand contributes to your overall sewing productivity. You can get the most out of any inventory control strategy by generalizing your purchases. For example, keep good supplies of ivory and black thread on hand; use the ivory to sew all light fabrics and the black to sew dark fabrics, instead of purchasing perfectly matching thread for every outfit. Alternatively, buy matching thread for the needle and use your basic neutral threads in the bobbin. Another example is to generalize your interfacing needs. Experiment with the different types until you find a lightweight, medium-weight, and heavyweight interfacing you like. Then, purchase several yards of each of the three weights a couple times a year, instead of purchasing small amounts every time you shop for a garment. An added benefit of generalizing your selection of supplies is that it saves money, trips to the sewing shop, and storage space!

IMPROVISE STORAGE

One of the best things about sewing is accumulating beautiful fabric, useful notions, and inspiring patterns. One of the worst is finding space to put it all. But don't despair—ideas for ingenious storage are almost infinite and can adapt to any situation. As mentioned above, rolling shelf units are immensely handy, and they can double as a base for a cutting surface. Stacking plastic baskets can hold lots of trims, supplies, and notions, and they can be stored under tables and at the bottom of closets. You can store fabrics on a shelf in the linen closet or hang them in garment bags in the closet, along with the family clothing. Or roll yardage on tubes recycled from fabric or upholstery shops and stand the rolls upright in a basket, just like they do at the stores.

Patterns can be saved in plastic reclosable bags, file folders, or manila clasp envelopes and stowed away in milk crates, cardboard boxes, or file storage boxes available from moving companies. Interfacings can be rolled on cardboard tubes left over from wrapping paper, folded into mesh laundry bags along with the plastic instruction sheet, or hung from skirt hangers, so you can easily find the one you need. Stacking boxes, shoe boxes, picnic baskets, and office supply filing cabinets can all be put to good use in the sewing area. Pegboard, spool racks, bobbin cases, and lots of other ingenious storage items are available at sewing stores, but keep your eyes open at the home improvement centers and hardware stores for good ideas on how to improvise storage. Plastic tubs for camping gear or toy storage, wastebaskets, and closet organizers can serve you well, too.

MAKE A "TO GO" SEWING KIT

In addition to the basic storage system for all your sewing stuff, it's essential to have a sewing kit that's always ready to pick up and go. A fishing tackle box, attaché case, carpenter's tool box, make-up kit, photographer's camera bag, or multi-purpose tote basket with small compartments are all good choices for a ready-set-go approach to sewing. Carry it to the cutting area, keep it nearby when marking fabric, and set it next to you when hemming the finished garment.

A Stitch in Time

No matter how small your sewing area is, try to incorporate some photos, drawings, or swatches from your inspiration files. Having them visible keeps the creative juices flowing and helps you come up with ideas for new projects or solutions.

Look in the sewing stores for ideas, but don't be afraid to improvise with carryalls designed for other purposes.

Once you have decided on a to-go carryall, keep it stocked with pins, needles, measuring tape, scissors, notepaper and pens, marking chalk or pencils, thimble, and the various other supplies you always need. Add the special notions required for a specific garment, such as the zipper or beads for embellishment, but remember to put these notions back into basic storage when you've completed the garment. This keeps your mobile sewing kit current, rather than weighed down with leftover supplies from past projects. Make sure it's handy, too, so you can grab it as you head out for an evening meeting or next door to visit a neighbor.

ATTEND TO THE DETAILS

Even though we're talking about creating the most efficient sewing area in the space you've got available, try to find room for the small details that make sewing an extra pleasant way to spend your time. A small radio, tape player, or television can keep you company. A favorite photograph or family memento is always comforting to look at, especially if you don't have a window or nice view. A clock will keep you (and dinner) on schedule; some sewers even use a kitchen timer, so they don't even have to waste the millisecond it takes to look up at a clock! A potpourri sachet, antique needle case, pretty ceramic dish (use it to hold your pins), or foot-warmer under the table all help to make your sewing area a comfortable and favorite place to be.

This is a great time in history to enjoy sewing because there are so many new tools and supplies that make it easier to sew more and sew better. On one of your shopping jaunts, take a few extra minutes to stroll through the notions and equipment departments of your favorite sewing store, or look over the "Quick Tour" of G Street Fabrics' supply departments on page 32 . You'll be fascinated with the many new items coming out all the time, and you may wonder how you managed to keep your head in the sand for so long. Don't get stuck in a habitual rut of doing things the same old way—explore the alternatives.

If you can't upgrade your sewing machine, and most of us can't very often, you should still be aware of how machine technology is developing. If your local dressmaker or a neighbor has a brand new machine that can do beautiful embroidery, you might be able to get some help with a trouble spot on an embroidered garment, for a small fee or in exchange for a similar favor. Besides, it's just fun to see what these machines can do. And if you have your eye on a new machine that is perfect for the kind of sewing you do, you can watch for sales and special deals that might take a bite out of the purchase price.

Most sewing machine companies also manufacture plenty of accessories and attachments, and you'll want to keep up with these, too. Your brand's company might come out with a super-duper buttonhole attachment that fits your machine and makes buttonholes a breeze—you won't want to miss out on it because you didn't know about it. Or there may be a special pin-tucking

attachment or sewing machine foot that cuts time and does a better job. Such attachments can reduce the overall time you spend on a project, not to mention the stress of doing things by hand or with limited equipment.

ACCESSORIES THAT INCREASE EFFICIENCY

Your review of the notions department at your favorite store or a sewing supply mail order catalog will probably introduce you to some new and strange accessories. You might not even know what some of them are for. But if you ask a few questions and study them closely, you might find that they will come in very handy on a particular project or inspire you to explore new sewing territory.

Newly developed notions make nearly every stage of sewing faster, easier, and more efficient. For pinning and cutting, you'll find all types of weights for holding pattern pieces down, removable or washable tape for temporary "pinning," and rotary cutters that speed along the pattern outlines in a flash. Versatile pens, pencils, and chalk devices help you accurately mark patterns and fabrics, and they even brush off or disappear by themselves so you don't have to worry about permanent stains. They also eliminate the need for time-consuming hand-done tailor tacks, so you finish at the cutting table and get to the sewing machine fast.

Fusibles and other methods of adhering fabric have quite simply revolutionized sewing. From interfacings to stabilizers, fabric glue to washable adhesive tapes and webs, the concept of stitching today means much more than just pins, needles, and thread. A spot of fabric glue to hold two pieces together temporarily can take the place of pinning and basting. Fusible inter-

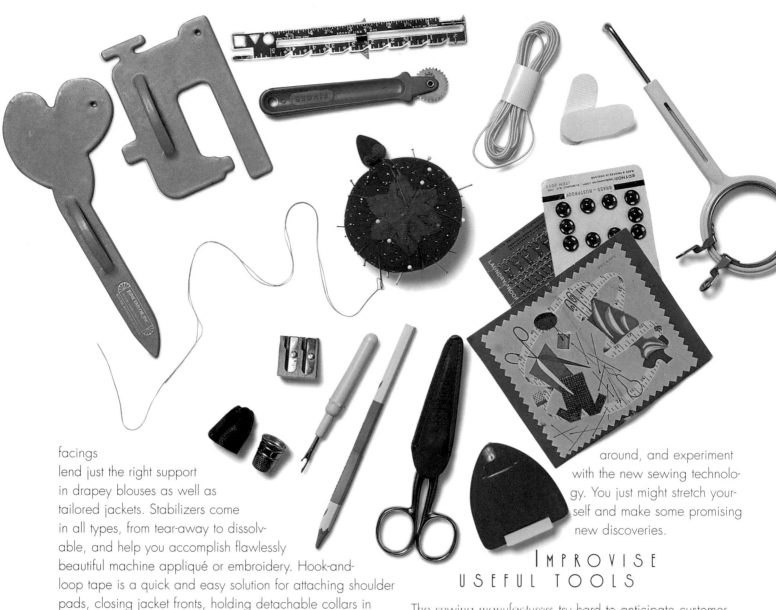

facings
lend just the right support
in drapey blouses as well as
tailored jackets. Stabilizers come
in all types, from tear-away to dissolv-
able, and help you accomplish flawlessly
beautiful machine appliqué or embroidery. Hook-and-
loop tape is a quick and easy solution for attaching shoulder
pads, closing jacket fronts, holding detachable collars in
place, and many other uses.

Different pressing aids help you achieve perfect points and
seams. Grid-marked sewing aids make easy work of maintaining accurate dimensions. Bias tape makers
and pocket templates create

customized
shapes and trims.
Assorted measuring tools are
designed for many different tasks.
Lending libraries of videos help you mas-
ter special techniques. Sewing shops offer bigger and better
selections of skill-sharpening classes. There are so many
resources out there to help you become a better, faster sewer
and to inspire you to try new techniques. So dive in, look

around, and experiment
with the new sewing technology. You just might stretch yourself and make some promising
new discoveries.

IMPROVISE
USEFUL TOOLS

The sewing manufacturers try hard to anticipate customer
needs and develop new products to satisfy them, but there's
no reason why you can't do the same. Just as you impro-
vised storage ideas, you can look around the house or hardware store and put existing tools to new uses in the sewing
room. You probably will save some money, too!

A Stitch in Time

Keep track of your notions and supplies, so
you won't run out of something essential just
when you need it. Periodic shopping trips
ensure that your supply needs are met.

From cans to clothespins, tweezers to toothbrushes, look for unusual and makeshift accessories. Tuna and cat food cans make great weights for holding patterns in place on the cutting table. Small woodworkers' clamps and clothespins are perfect for holding things in place. Cotton swabs, gentle computer vacuums, and artists' paintbrushes are adaptable machine cleaning aids that get into cramped spaces. Kitchen matches and toothpicks can be used as spacers for sewing on buttons. Needle-nose pliers from the workshop get a grip on stubborn thread ends. Fishing weights and buckshot add heft to a hem. Toothbrushes brush away chalk markings in a second. Tweezers can zero in precisely on small areas and short threads. A lazy Susan stores notions in an easy-to-reach fashion. Jewelry and art supplies, dental and medical equipment, computer tools, and common household items can all be cross-trained to work out in the sewing room.

KNOW WHAT YOUR EQUIPMENT CAN DO

You probably are pretty good friends with your sewing machine, but you should take the time to know it intimately. That means learning about all parts on the machine and every little thing it's capable of doing. Reread the owner's manual every so often, to remind yourself of those bonus attractions of the machine, such as built-in needle threaders, clippers, or seam allowance guides. Then make up practice samples of every stitch or stitch variation, so you can see at a glance which ones might add something special to a garment you're planning. You might want to compile a scrapbook of samples of all of your machine's stitches, along with notes about stitch width, length, needle and bobbin tension, or other details that are important to remember. This scrapbook will be a resource guide for you in the future, when you want to know how a particular stitch looks on a particular fabric or you can't quite remember how you set up the machine for a certain effect.

Whenever you purchase new tools or improvise them, be sure you study all of their capabilities. You'll get the most benefit from accessories that you learn how to use completely, taking advantage of all of their features. So read the instructions, ask questions of your favorite store's sales staff, and experiment on your own. You'll end up saving time because you'll know exactly what your equipment can do and which accessories will provide the assistance you need.

KEEP YOUR EQUIPMENT IN TIP-TOP SHAPE

Sewing downtime because of equipment failure is a big time-consumer and an even greater disappointment. When you're fired up to sew and your machine goes on the blitz, tears can flow and hearts can break. So don't wait until crisis hits—take steps to keep your equipment in the best possible shape. Follow the same preventive care philosophy you use for your family's health care or auto maintenance. Review your equipment owner manuals or check with your sewing dealer for a recommended "tune-up" maintenance schedule and follow those guidelines. Learn how to take care of your equipment and it will take care of you—providing you with hours of trouble-free, on-demand sewing.

A Stitch in Time

Don't forget your own comfort when you sew. A well-designed chair will support you comfortably and good lights will keep you alert for hours of productive sewing time.

Strolling the aisles of G Street Fabrics, near Washington, D.C., will reveal these labor-saving (and time-saving!) treasures. Most of them are also available at sewing and fabric shops near you, or through the mail order sewing supply catalogs. Experiment with new sewing notions to find those that will help you sew faster and better.

FUSIBLE WEB PRODUCTS

These come in strips of various strengths and widths, and can be used to fuse hems (especially recommended for fabrics such as Ultrasuede, which shows pinholes forever), fuse seams (thus eliminating the need for sewing), and for adhering multiple layers and appliqués. Some varieties have paper backing, which allow them to be fused first to one layer and then to another, after removing the backing. Brand names include Stitch Witchery, Heat 'n Bond, and Wonder Under.

FUSIBLE INTERFACINGS, THERMAL FLEECE, AND OTHER BATTING

These come in wovens (ranging from lightweight to canvas), nonwovens (in a range of weights), knits (from lightweight to medium weight), thermal linings, and quilting batts. Fusible interfacings are especially helpful to add support to facings, buttonholes, welt pockets, and other tailored details (thus eliminating the need for tedious pad stitching).

ELASTIC PLEATING TAPE

This is a woven fabric band, in 1½" (4 cm) or 2¼" (5.5 cm) width, that is threaded with multiple rows of elastic. The band can be sewn to the wrong side of a waistband, and the elastic threads drawn up to quickly produce multiple rows of gathering.

Other special waistband elastics and interfacings are available to make sewing waistbands easier and mistake-proof.

GRIDDED SELF-HEALING PLASTIC CUTTING MATS

These come in several sizes and are very helpful for laying out a pattern and determining the straight of grain. The mats are also handy as tabletop protectors when using a rotary cutter, which are much faster than scissors, cut a cleaner edge, and are easier on your hands. Using a self-healing ruler with a rotary cutter turns out straight strips in a breeze.

WASHAWAY WONDER TAPE®

This double-sided transparent tape can be used to baste and/or stabilize a seam. It doesn't have to be removed after stitching, as it washes completely away with the first laundering. A non-washable type is also available, which can be placed adjacent to the seamline as a basting substitute and then removed.

WASH-AWAY, TEAR-AWAY, AND BURN-AWAY STABILIZERS

These products add greater stability and support to buttonholes, decorative stitching, and free-motion machine embroidery or quilting, depending on the fabric's care requirements. After stitching, they can be torn, washed, or burned (more literally, ironed) away.

SEAMS GREAT® NYLON TRANSPARENT TAPE

Available in ⅝" (1.5 cm) width and various colors, this can be a lifesaver when working with lightweight fabrics that fray easily. Use it to cover the raw edges of the seam, thus reinforcing and finishing the seam in one step. Also useful for serged and rolled edges on lightweight fabric.

HOOK-AND-EYE AND SNAP TAPES

These tapes are quick and easy substitutes for buttons or zippers in long closures. They are sold by the yard in black or white, which can be dyed.

BRIDAL BUTTON LOOPS

Love the look of a zillion buttons, but hate the thought of creating all those tiny button loops? This tape is sold by the yard, giving you as many loops as you need. It is also useful for attaching feather trim that must be removed for cleaning.

BUTTONEER TOOL®

A gadget for attaching or reattaching four-holed buttons without having to sew them.

BUTTON PINS

These look like hump-backed safety pins; the hump is designed to go through the button shank when the pin is inserted from the wrong side. Good for shank buttons that must be removed for cleaning or to attach buttons when you don't have time to sew them on.

HOT GLUE GUN

A staple supply for craft-making, this tool is a very simple and quick way to attach embellishments.

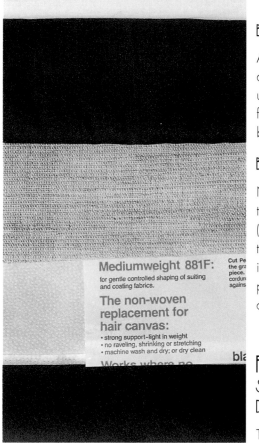

Mediumweight 881F:
for gentle controlled shaping of suiting and coating fabrics.

The non-woven replacement for hair canvas:
- strong support–light in weight
- no raveling, shrinking or stretching
- machine wash and dry; or dry clean

bla

Works where no

BIAS TAPE MAKER

A simple tool available in a variety of sizes and used to double-fold fabric strips for custom-made bias tape.

BIAS BUDDY®

No more burnt hands with this invention! Thread the folded bias strip (perhaps made with the above tool) through the Bias Buddy and place iron right on top to iron the folds in place. Can be set for various widths of bias tape.

FROM THE SEWING MACHINE DEPARTMENT:

This is where the miracles of new technology can amaze and delight you. Sergers manufactured for home use and computerized sewing machines have truly revolutionized home sewing. Whether or not you can replace your machine, it's fun to see what the new models can do.

SERGERS

The serger is to the sewing room what the microwave is to the kitchen. A serger won't replace your traditional sewing machine, but it can be a great complement. It does only a

A Stitch in Time

Explore and experiment with new developments in the field. Watch the new sewing machine demonstrations, study the capabilities of new attachments, and try out the new sewing aids to see which advances in technology will help you advance your skills.

few things, but does them incredibly well and fast. Sergers sew, overcast, trim, and finish a seam all in one operation. The resulting seam, especially when stitched with four threads, is both strong and stretchy—making the serger the machine of choice for knits and stretch fabrics. Most models also sew a beautiful rolled edge and some feature a chain stitch, super-stretchy two-thread seam, and decorative stitch for a visible hem on knits. Threading and tension-setting can be tricky, so unless you are mechanically adept, purchase a serger from a reputable dealer who will provide guide classes on its operation.

EMBROIDERY MACHINES, SCANNERS, AND COMPUTER SOFTWARE

Preprogrammed with alphabets, monograms, and large-scale embroidery designs, these machines run themselves once you have threaded them and made your selection. If the design calls for several colors, the machine will patiently wait until you are free to change the thread. The scanners and software enable you to create your own designs or combine and alter the built-in ones. Some embroidery machines can even interface with your home computer to produce the designs you create with graphics software.

NEEDLE STOP DOWN

This features puts the needle down in the fabric when you take your foot off the pedal, freeing you from having to adjust the needle position with the hand wheel. Good for free-motion embroidery or other operations that require lots of pivoting.

PRESSER FOOT KNEE LEVER

Raise or lower the presser foot with a lever next to your knee, so you can keep your hands on the fabric.

BUILT-IN INVISIBLE HEMSTITCH

Even the least expensive machines include this stitch, but they may not provide the special foot that comes with higher priced models; the foot ensures that the hem is truly invisible. The machine-sewn hem has perfectly adjusted tightness to eliminate puckering, is less likely to unravel, and is a lot faster than a hand-sewn hem.

BUILT-IN BUTTONHOLES

Standard on more and more sewing machines; some computerized models memorize the length, density, and shape (rectangular, keyhole, or eyelet) that you set for the buttonhole and then repeat it as many times as you wish without resetting. Special buttonhole feet are also available to ease correct measurement.

RUFFLE ATTACHMENT

If you make dust ruffles or full petticoats, this attachment will quickly pay for itself. The attachment makes tiny tucks in the fabric and attaches it to a flat piece in one operation. Not suitable for gathers that must be adjusted before attaching to another fabric piece.

PIPING FEET

These sewing machine feet are available in several sizes and facilitate the creation and application of impeccable piping. Much easier than using a zipper foot.

A Stitch in Time

Improvise accessories by putting household items, computer tools, jewelry and woodworking supplies to work for you—from cat food cans as pattern weights to tiny jeweler's tweezers for pulling thread ends.

COUCHING FEET

These sewing machine feet have clever little tunnels through which cords or strings of beads can pass; they are held in place while you anchor them with zigzag stitches.

Ask your sewing machine dealer about other specialty feet for your sewing machine or serger. Many different models are available, designed for many different purposes—perhaps some will make your sewing projects easier to stitch and faster to complete.

MARY MORRIS IS AN ENTHUSIASTIC SEWER, THE PATTERN AND BOOK BUYER FOR G STREET FABRICS, AND CO-AUTHOR OF *EVERY SEWER'S GUIDE TO THE PERFECT FIT: CUSTOMIZING YOUR PATTERNS FOR A SENSATIONAL LOOK.*

G E T   R E A D Y
G E T   S E T :
Preparation for efficient sewing

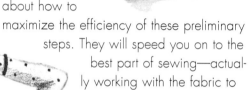

Once you've scheduled some time, found sources of inspiration, selected patterns and fabrics, organized the sewing area, and assembled useful tools and equipment, it's just about time to get set for sewing. However, you're not quite ready to sit down at the machine. Fabric preparation, pattern fitting, cutting, and marking all have to come first and are the preliminary steps that set the stage for successful sewing. Lots of sewers dread cutting and fitting, but you can approach these "get set" steps like anything else—in easily manageable segments of time that fit into your busy schedule. Read on for some suggestions about how to maximize the efficiency of these preliminary steps. They will speed you on to the best part of sewing—actually working with the fabric to create the beautiful garments you see in your mind's eye.

When you finally start sewing, you can take advantage of other efficient techniques that help you breeze through construction steps without mishaps and master those finishing touches that set your handmade originals apart. So, now that you're ready, get set to turn your limited sewing time into unlimited productivity and creativity.

You've probably heard the woodworker's expression, "Measure twice, cut once." These four simple words are a great reminder about taking extra care at the beginning of an important process, to make sure that the result you get is the one you want. Take the time getting ready up front, so you won't spend time later on correcting errors, saving disasters, or worse, having to purchase materials and start at the beginning all over again. Even though it's a woodworker's expression, it sure applies to sewing—and especially to fitting! In fact, we should all stitch it as a sampler and hang it up in the sewing area so it reminds us to check the pattern for good fit before we do anything else.

Sewing "war stories" always include tales about fitting problems, about spending the time to sew garments that don't fit right or trying to fix a poor-fitting garment and ending up with a total loss. We've all given these failures to the flea markets and used clothing stores of the world, and some of us have even tossed them in the garbage. The more clever and patient sewers among us have recycled parts of these sewing casualties into more successful "second wind" garments.

Regardless of the outcome, it is undeniably frustrating to spend precious money and even more precious time on sewing projects that end up somewhere other than the closet. Therefore, it's very important to learn something about altering patterns to fit your figure perfectly, or at least acceptably. You may be able to make just a few simple adjustments to every pattern you select in order to get fabulous-looking results. However, if your fitting challenges are significant, you may want to purchase a textbook on the subject or enroll in a serious pattern-fitting class at a local sewing shop or community college.

Either way you go, make sure you evaluate every pattern before you make it up. And then re-evaluate the pattern every time you make it again, just in case your measurements have changed or if you will be adding some creative touches that might adjust the way the pattern goes together. This important "prep step" will keep you from taking stitches out, redoing assembly steps, and perhaps even purchasing and recutting fabric for replacement pieces. Believe it or not, you will save time in the end by spending time in the beginning.

THE BOTTOM LINE: KNOW THE NUMBERS

Know what your own measurements are, honestly, and compare them to the measurements printed on the pattern envelope. Use the comparison as a guide to the types of alterations you may have to make. For example, your waist or hip measurement may not be remotely close to the pattern's waist or hip for your supposed size. Don't despair—not one of us conforms to the pattern companies' silhouettes. You might as well know what the differences are right at the beginning, so you can make adjustments before you start sewing. In the example above, you will know right at the outset that you will have to alter the waistline or hipline of the pattern to fit you.

Alternatively, cut the pattern pieces apart, measure the corresponding areas right on the tissue, and compare to your

A Stitch in Time

Knowing the numbers is not a game. An honest knowledge of your true measurements will help you fit patterns correctly for your very individual figure.

own figure. Study the pattern pieces and imagine how they will look on your individual body. You might want to pin them together to make a tissue half-dress and carefully put it on. Even though the tissue will not hang anything like fabric, it might indicate a serious fitting problem you wouldn't have known about until too late.

Before you cut into the fabric, make the pattern changes that will ensure a better fit, which automatically means a more beautiful-looking result. Multi-size patterns can be helpful here, by providing a number of cutting lines you can use to accommodate your variable measurements. Lowering the neckline for comfort, reducing the dart width to accommodate a generous tummy, adding walking ease to a front-opening garment, lengthening or shortening a skirt, and redrawing seamlines for various effects are among the many pattern alterations you might experiment with. And you can't deny that experimenting with them is a lot easier when you're still working with pattern tissue than with the fashion fabric.

MAKE A SAMPLE

Like many sewers, you might groan when you hear the advice, "Make a muslin." When you've got limited time to begin with, you want to spend it sewing gorgeous new garments out of the fantastic new fabrics you purchased. The notion of first making the dress out of boring old muslin can be enough to drive you out of the house screaming, "I'll never get any sewing done!" But, here again, a little time spent up front saves redo time later, not to mention the agony of that moment in front of the mirror when you realize the finished garment does not fit. Thankfully, muslin is very inexpen-

sive and easy to get. Making a muslin may lead you to the discovery that the pattern you selected will not give you the desired result. Therefore, you can select another pattern or combine it with a different fabric.

If you grit your teeth and agree to make a muslin first, just breeze through it. Indicate the notches, assembly tips, and any other hints with chalk or marker right on the cut-out pattern pieces so you won't have to refer to the printed pattern instructions. Set the sewing machine to the longest stitch length, so you'll fly through the seams. You can be speedy, but do try to stitch accurate seam allowances. Use up thread on old bobbins to avoid thread waste, to clean off the bobbins, and so you don't waste time rethreading the machine for a garment you'll never wear. Don't bother basting or stay-stitching. Just get the muslin garment together as quickly as possible so you can evaluate the fit and make changes before you cut into the real fabric. By the way, you can recycle old muslin garments, cutting up the major pieces for other patterns that need to be tested.

Do not skimp on pressing the muslin garment, no matter what streamlined methods you use to assemble it! The pattern will not come out right, and you just cannot evaluate the final fit unless seams, darts, and other features are correctly pressed as you complete them. Sewing the entire garment together and then trying to press it just won't cut it (no pun intended), and the whole purpose of making a muslin will have been futile.

An alternative to making the muslin is to pre-test the pattern in a very inexpensive "test" fabric that, if the pattern comes out great, you could actually wear. If you go this route, you will have to be more careful with cutting, marking, and assembly. But you'll have the bonus of ending up with a wearable dress that started out as just a sample.

A Stitch in Time

If patterns never fit you right, have a look at a good book on fitting or think about enrolling in a fitting class. Once you learn what alterations you have to make to a pattern, your garments will come out perfectly every time.

FITTING DURING ASSEMBLY

Do review the fit as you put the garment together. Baste difficult steps, such as sleeve insertions, and try on before you sew. You might as well know as soon as possible if there are especially tricky steps or if the sleeves will be too tight or short, for example. Use a dress form, if you've got one, to test the fit as you go, or wear easy-to-remove clothing and try the garment on often.

A Stitch in Time

You'll feel free to move around if you add walking ease to the front opening of dresses, jackets, and coats. The little bit of extra fabric keeps the garment from spreading open when you walk. See Figure 1 on page 118 for the how-to steps.

A Stitch in Time

The woodworker's expression advises,
"Measure twice, cut once."
It's true for sewing, too!

Checking the fit as you go will ensure a perfect result, and you'll spend a lot less time ripping out stitches. Besides, trying on the garment gives you the opportunity to get up from your sewing chair, move around, stretch a bit, have an inspiring look at the fabric for your next project, or kiss the dog—plenty of reasons to be glad you reevaluated the fit throughout the construction process.

Preparing the materials

Preshrinking, marking, and cutting fabric are the least favorite steps for a lot of sewers. Dreaming about different patterns is fun, buying the fabric is exciting, sewing the garment is satisfying, and wearing the finished item is fulfilling. However, the stages between buying the fabric and sewing the pattern pieces together seem to take so long and are so dull. But you can speed through these intermediate steps by working them into your regular schedule and completing them as efficiently as possible.

Evaluate your weekly schedule for available time slots, and put each day to use to make progress on sewing prep steps as well as garment assembly. Each designer dress in this book features a *Plan for the Week*, which breaks down the entire assembly process into manageable daily tasks and ensures that the dress will be completed on the weekend. You can put together the same plan for all the projects you undertake. For example, if you select a pattern and purchase some fabric on a *Monday* during lunch hour, start prewashing the fabric that evening before dinner and study the pattern steps after dinner. On *Tuesday* evening, make any desired design changes, referring to your inspiration sources for ideas, and alter the pattern if necessary for improved fit. On *Wednesday* evening, mark and cut out the fabric and interfacing, and experiment with your sewing machine's different decorative stitches for some embroidery on the collar and cuffs. On *Thursday*, fuse all interfacing in place and start working on the machine

embroidery. On *Friday* evening, begin stitching the garment and complete the embroidery. On *Saturday*, finish assembling the garment. On *Sunday*, complete the finishing touches—buttons, snaps, hemming, etc.

As you can see, planning ahead is extremely valuable here, just as it is when thinking about patterns and fabrics. And once you start, you'll discover new ways to efficiently schedule all the steps and stages of the sewing process. For example, if you're planning to sew up three new dresses for summer, work on them all at the same time instead of completing one before starting another. Think about using the same pattern for all three and distinguish each version with creative design ideas or embellishment possibilities—the final section of this book highlights this approach to diversifying standard patterns. Then, you can layer the three fabrics and cut out the three dresses as one. If you choose a temperamental fabric, however, don't try to layer it with another. Instead, cut the dresses separately and do the marking in assembly-line fashion.

Alternatively, take a seasonal approach and sew the three different dresses for spring, summer, and fall. This is a great strategy for making the most of limited sewing time, and for building a year-round wardrobe. Keep all components for the different dresses in stacking baskets or separate bins, along with their accompanying notions, buttons, trims, and accessories. Proceed with the marking, interfacing, and sewing in assembly-line fashion, switching from one dress to the other. Setting yourself up to be efficient in this way speeds your sewing, and produces new additions to your wardrobe at a faster rate.

A Stitch in Time

Spend some time pretreating fabrics at the beginning to save time solving problems later on. Prewashed fabrics and trims don't surprise you with shrinking and puckering in the finished garment.

PRETREATING THE FABRIC

It's tempting to bring beautiful new fabric home from the store and cut right into it, but try to hold back just a little while. The brief time spent pretreating fabric will save lots of time later on, when you might otherwise be faced with a garment that has shrunk in unflattering places after being washed. Pretreating also helps remove chemicals and fabric finishes left by the manufacturing process and makes the yardage easier to handle. Yes, this preparation takes time

A Stitch in Time

Work the fabric prep steps into your daily schedule. Prewash new yardage in between loads of the family laundry or while you're completing other get-ready stages like evaluating your pattern, making design changes, or experimenting with a decorative stitch swatch.

exactly when you're most excited to get started sewing, but if you build it into a larger sewing schedule, it won't feel like a delay. Besides, while you are preshrinking, you can be completing other prep steps such as making creative design changes to the pattern, adjusting fitting alterations, or experimenting with decorative stitch swatches to work out your sewing plan.

When you purchase fabric, check the bolt ends for care instructions or ask your sewing dealer for tips about how to clean the cloth. Don't forget to ask about shrinkage! This is another reason to jot down notes about the fabric you buy, such as how many yards you purchased, how to care for it, and how much it can be expected to shrink. If the fabric salesperson reports that the yardage is likely to shrink 4" (10 cm) per yard when washed, you will want to purchase enough extra to cover this shrinkage allowance. You may even be advised to prewash the fabric more than once, to be sure all shrinkage has occurred before you cut it out. Few things in life are as discouraging as finding out, after pretreating the fabric, that you're 1/8 yard (.15 m) short. At times like these, the fabric store always seems to sell out fast. If you do run a bit short and the fabric is long gone from the store, don't worry. It's just another opportunity to be creative.

You've heard the expression, "Necessity is the mother of invention." It probably originated with a frustrated seamstress, who didn't have quite enough yardage to make her dream dress. See page 56 for tips about saving disasters, including how to make a yardage miscalculation seem as if you planned it.

Before the yardage actually goes into the washing machine or sink, serge or overcast the raw edges to keep the threads from unraveling and getting tangled. Yes, it's yet another advance step, but why lose a precious 1" (2.5 cm) of fabric? Also, mark the right side of the fabric with a colored thread loop or safety pin. It's a lot easier to identify the right side when the fabric is fresh from the bolt than when it comes out of the wash. If you're not sure exactly which side is the right side, ask the sewing salesperson when the yardage is cut. If both sides look identical to you, it may not be important to distinguish right side from wrong side. However, in this case, make sure you select and identify a "right" side when cutting out the pattern, so the garment pieces will go together correctly.

A general rule for fabric preparation is to pretreat the uncut yardage in the same fashion as you will care for the finished garment. In other words, if you plan to make up a machine-washable cotton dress, preshrink the cotton yardage in the washing machine on the appropriate settings. If you purchase a fine silk, you may be able to machine wash both the uncut material and the finished garment on a delicate cycle or wash by hand.

Be aware that a "Dry Clean Only" fabric will not sew up into a machine-washable garment, no matter how careful you are. You will most likely have to dry clean the finished

A Stitch in Time

Take the guesswork out of garment maintenance by finding out how to care for a fabric before you leave the store. Check the ends of the bolts or ask the salesperson about the recommended care instructions—and make a note of it so you won't forget by the time you're ready to cut and sew.

item, so have the yardage preshrunk at the dry cleaners. Alternatively, improvise a pretreatment method by spritzing the cloth with warm water and hanging it to dry, or hanging the yardage in a hot, steamy bathroom. Some sewers do not preshrink dry-cleanable fabric at all before cutting and sewing, so go by your own experience and judgment here. With the exception of a stretchy fabric, such as wool crepe, you can pretty safely assume that a finished dry-cleanable garment assembled without pretreating the fabric will not shrink noticeably after dry cleaning.

Try to coordinate pretreating activities with your normal laundering schedule. You can mix a few yards of cotton denim into the same load as family clothes, or sneak a small load of newly purchased fabric in between regular family loads. If you're nervous about mixing brand new fabric with well-worn clothes, then cut a healthy swatch off the yardage and throw it in the laundry with everything else. At least you'll find out in advance how it behaves, and then you can prewash the fabric by itself with confidence.

If you stockpile fabrics for future sewing projects and keep notes about pretreating requirements for specific pieces, go ahead and preshrink different pieces of yardage together. Even if you're not ready to sew or don't yet know what you'll be making out of it, the fabric will be ready and waiting when you are set to go. You might want to schedule part of an evening or weekend day just for preshrinking groups of interfacings, linings, and other notions. Then, if you need just ¼ yard (.25 m) of interfacing and you're in a rush to complete the next assembly step, you'll know it has already been pretreated. You won't be tempted to skip this important step and then have to live with the puckered results in the finished collar or cuffs.

PREPARING THE PATTERN

While your fabric and interfacings are drying, use the time to review the sewing pattern again and get it ready. Press the pattern pieces with a barely warm, dry iron to get out the wrinkles so it will lay flat for accurate cutting. Familiarize yourself with the location of notches and other important marks, as well as which pieces will need interfacing. Review any alterations you made to the pattern pieces so that nothing will slip by unnoticed during the cutting and marking stages. Look over the pattern instructions, especially the cutting layouts, so you won't waste any time when your fabric is dry and ready to cut into. And, finally, scan the pattern pieces and instructions once more, looking for opportunities to make a creative alteration or to add some special flair. Note them on the pattern instruction sheets at the appropriate points, so you'll remember any adjustments in cutting or sewing you'll have to make.

CUTTING AND MARKING

Before you lay out the pattern pieces on the fabric, take a
moment to reacquaint yourself with the amount of yardage,
the right and wrong sides of the fabric, and the recommended layout for the pattern you're making. Also, check that the
grain is straight, or "true," that the
selvages are evenly aligned, and
that the
fabric
lays flat
on your
cut-

ting
surface.
Assemble your sup-
plies, including pattern, scissors, measuring tape, pins or
weights, notepad and pen, munchies and beverage, plus
whatever else you need to avoid running back and forth
from cutting table to sewing storage area. Scan the pattern
once more, to make sure you're clear about what version
you're cutting out and what design or construction changes
you'll be making.

If convenient, set up your cutting area in front of the television or in the family room, so you'll have some company.
Or play your favorite music to make the task more pleasant.
Time-saving and labor-saving tools will keep you from taking
too many shortcuts at this critical stage of sewing. Review

the *Quick Tour of the Notions and Supply Department* on
page 32 for ideas about speedy cutting and marking
accessories, or ask your sewing dealer for some tips to
make this stage go faster.

Pattern markings help you align the garment sections correctly, so it's very important that you transfer all of the various
dots and notches to the fabric. This is especially important if
you're cutting several garments at once and it will be a
while before you start assembling them. Don't depend too
much on your memory to help you put the pattern together
correctly. Your memory will probably disappoint you, and
you'll waste time getting out all the pattern pieces to review
the location of important dots and alignment marks. Pattern
layouts also tell you whether the pieces should be right side
up or not, how they should relate to grainlines, and whether
you need to pay attention to fabric nap or diagonals. These
are all important considerations, and you probably have disaster stories of your own about cutting mishaps, so depend
on your own experience for guidance.

When you're finished cutting the fashion fabric, go ahead
and get the lining and interfacings cut out, instead of waiting until you need them. Don't forget to save a few scraps of
fashion fabric and interfacing, so you can fuse or baste
together some test pieces. These interfaced scraps come in
very handy later on, when you need to evaluate stitch quality, test machine embroidery motifs, or make buttonhole samples. Scraps are also useful for last-minute appliqué motifs,
button loops, covered buttonholes, or (alas!) patches to
mend an accidental tear or clip made in the wee hours by
sleepy hands.

Before disassembling your cutting area, make sure you have
cut out and marked everything you'll need for the upcoming
garment or garments. Then, stow all cut fabric pieces (along
with a few extra scraps, just in case), pattern contents, and
any notes you made during the cutting/marking process all
together in the same basket or bin.

Get ready, get set ... S E W !

Here comes the best part about sewing—actually sitting down at the machine and working with the fabric. You've planned your time, prepared the fabric, decided on the special touches you will add to the pattern, and organized your space. You now **deserve** to have a seat and enjoy yourself—let someone else answer the phone, wash the dishes, or walk the dog. You've worked hard for this moment, so don't let it pass you by.

By now, you probably know the pattern instructions for your dress pretty well, especially if you've made it up before. However, scan the assembly steps one more time and look for ways you can save time or further increase efficiency. Perhaps you'll see how you can reorganize the assembly process for any number of reasons—to get the least favorite steps done first, group similar types of procedures, or coordinate the process with the amount of time you have available to sew. For example, you might pick out certain stages of the dress construction and complete them in one session. If you've only got an hour to sew, look for the construction steps that can be fully completed in that time; it's disorienting to stop in midstream, and it always feels better to finish something before you turn off the machine for the night. Whatever assembly system you use, trust your own experience and feel free to reorganize the order of construction steps. Learn to look at the pattern as a set of suggested instructions, not a mandate to follow them exactly. If your experience leads you to follow a slightly different path, trust your instincts.

Make notes on the pattern to remind yourself where you might be diverging from the instructions. If the creative touch you will be adding to the pattern requires that you remember to stop between assembly steps 4 and 5, in order to complete the innovation, don't trust it to your memory. Make a note right on the pattern paper where you will stop, or use a Post-It note, paper clip, or other marker to alert you. You'll save aggravating minutes of ripping out and backing up to the point where you are making a change to the pattern.

EFFICIENT SEWING TECHNIQUES

If you have been sewing for any length of time, you probably know of all kinds of tips and hints for time-saving and labor-saving sewing. Draw upon your own knowledge to make the most of the time you have or review the "A Stitch in Time" boxes throughout this book and in other resources in your sewing library to brush up on tricks of the trade that help you sew better and faster.

A good basic starting point for efficient sewing is to work with the garment as flat as possible. In other words, try to hold off sewing underarm and side seams as long as possible because it's quicker to stitch straight seams than in rounds or along curves. Group straight pieces together and stitch them in assembly-line fashion, one right after another, without clipping the thread in between. Just stitch a thread chain for an inch or so between the pieces and cut them all apart when you're through.

Another good basic rule is to group similar types of construction together. For example, both the collar and cuffs usually require interfacing, stitching, clipping, turning, and pressing. However, construction of the collar usually comes early in the pattern instructions and the cuffs usually are near the end. Do them at the same time and set the cuffs aside for when you get to the sleeves—it will be a welcome treat to know that the cuffs are ready and waiting.

A Stitch in Time

To save time, cut out several sewing projects at once, layered one on top of another or in assembly-line fashion. Stow all the components— pattern, cut-out fabric and interfacing, thread, swatch samples, zipper, buttons, and notions—in separate boxes or bins.

USE ALL AVAILABLE RESOURCES

Your sewing machine can be a partner in efficiency, so try to learn its features that can help you maximize productivity. For example, select a long stitch or automatic basting feature to speedily assemble pieces so you can try them on and evaluate the fit. Turn the stitch length dial all the way down to zero to secure the threads at the beginning and ends of seams, or backstitch a bit with very short stitches (don't forget to turn the stitch length back to normal). Use the built-in needle threaders, thread clippers, measuring aids, and free arm—the sewing machine designers put them there to assist you.

If you're lucky enough to have a serger as well as a standard sewing machine, use them both. The serger makes fast work of stitching and trimming straight seams on its own, as well as finishing seam edges sewn on the standard machine. Make notes on your pattern sheets to remind you which machine to use for maximum efficiency.

Browse the notions department and hardware store for products to help speed sewing. For example, clothespins can hold seams in place while you stitch, new adhesive products can cut down basting time, and hook-and-loop tape can substitute for complicated closures.

SHED SOME LIGHT

One of the most important contributors to productive sewing is good light. Although the built-in lights featured on most sewing machines and sergers are very convenient, they usually are not strong enough for good visibility. Clamp-on lamps attached to your sewing table or movable stand-up lamps that can be positioned just right will help you see what you're doing and cut down on fatigue. This is critical if you're sewing in the evening after a long day or you're working with dark fabric and thread. That dark thread can just disappear into the fabric and, without good light, you may end up clipping or pulling something you'll wish you hadn't.

PRESSING IMPORTANCE

While you're breezing along on the sewing machines, it may seem like a big inconvenience to have to stop, get up, turn on the iron, and wait for it to heat up—just to press one seam. However, **do not** cut this corner. Pressing a garment as you construct it is crucial to the good fit and look of the final product. This is why it's helpful to group construction steps and stitch more than one piece at a time, so you can

also press more than one piece at a time in assembly-line fashion. While the iron is heating up, do something else such as review the next step, pin or baste the seam you'll be sewing next, refresh your cold drink, or stretch your shoulders. Alternatively, leave the iron turned on during the entire sewing session so it will always be ready for you when you are ready for it. Just make sure you keep an eye on the water level, if you're steam-pressing.

Once the garment pieces are pressed, try to keep them flat or drape them on a dress form. The less you handle the fabric, the better; garment pieces won't stretch out of shape and you'll have an easier time getting seams to match up correctly. As the garment goes together, put it on a hanger or dress form between sewing sessions. After you have so carefully stitched and pressed it, you won't want to come back to a crumpled pile the next evening and have to redo any steps. It's also a good idea to let the garment hang 24 hours, or at least overnight, before hemming, so the fabric and line of the garment can settle into place. This is especially important for stretchy fabrics and garments made on the bias, which can easily stretch out of shape if not allowed to relax.

While on the subject of the iron, it's a good time to repeat the difference between pressing and ironing. Pressing is just what the word says—a downward pressure with a bit of weight behind it. You don't move the iron back and forth, just press it down to open a seam, flatten a dart, or shape a design feature. Ironing is what you do with the tablecloth—move the iron back and forth to get the wrinkles out.

Your own sewing experience, or favorite sewing dealer, will be a trustworthy guide to the effective use of pressing aids for handling different fabrics. For example, tailor's hams and clappers help shape garments while you press them or trap steam in the fabric; velvet boards keep from crushing the nap; different tricks of the trade prevent the imprint of seam edges from showing on the right side. Check your own sewing room or the notions department of your favorite sewing store if you feel you need some accessories for effective pressing.

HAND STITCHING

Learning how to save time and increase efficiency is one of the basic goals of this book, so hand stitching probably seems like an odd subject to include. However, you can't deny that there is a place for handwork in every garment you make, from pre-basting a complex seam to tacking shoulder pads in place. Like every other stage of the sewing process, hand stitching can be organized for optimum productivity. Group different handwork projects and do them all at the same time, or use the hand-stitched step of garment construction as an opportunity to take a break from the sewing room and join the family in the den.

To save time when hand basting, use the same color of thread that you're using to construct the garment. If you've got good light, you'll be able to see where to sew and you may not have to pick out the basting thread. Alternatively, use a contrasting thread for easy visibility and baste adjacent to the seamline, not right on it, so you won't stitch over the basting thread and it will be easy to pull out.

RESPECT YOURSELF

You're probably not Superwoman, so don't be too demanding of yourself. If you've organized your sewing area, reserved the available slots of time in your busy schedule, prepared everything for maximum efficiency, and you manage to get some time at the machine every day, pat yourself on the back. Don't sew when you're tired or when another deadline is breathing down your neck—you'll risk making errors that can be even more frustrating.

When you first sit down at the sewing machine, glance at your pattern and set a goal. For example, say to yourself, "Tonight, I'll get the collar assembled and basted in place." Do that, and no more. You'll enjoy having completed something, and tomorrow you can move on to something else. If, after reaching your goal for the day, there's still some available time and you've got the energy, set another goal or do something else. Admire your fabric stash, review the next pattern on your "To Do" list, or make a buttonhole sample. All of these activities may or may not relate to the project you're working on at the moment, but they will require your attention at some time or another.

Before you call it quits, take a few moments to clean up and get set for the next sewing session. If it will require a change of machine needle and thread, make the change before you turn out the lights or gather the needed supplies and put them right by the machine. When you come back next time, everything will be ready for you. Make sure the iron and sewing machine are turned off. Cover the sewing machine, hang up the garment-in-progress, admire your expert stitching, and turn out the lights. Now you can look forward to your next visit.

The time you spend adding finishing touches to a dress can make the difference between a fabulous look and one that's just so-so. When you put some thought into the final details of your garment—before, during, and after sewing it—the result is a polished and put-together look that makes a lasting impression. The possibilities for innovative finishes are nearly infinite and can include buttons, trims, fabric sculpture, ascots and scarves, as well as accessories such as hats, jewelry, and gloves. The dresses featured later in this book illustrate a variety of ways to add a finishing touch that makes the fashion a true expression of your personal style.

PLAN AHEAD

This may sound redundant, but planning ahead for the particular finishing touches you will use saves time in the end and also ensures that the design accents are compatible in style with the overall garment. Right at the beginning, evaluate your pattern for elements of construction that can also provide design interest. For instance, consider splitting the pattern pieces apart to create opportunities for creative color-blocking or patchwork possibilities, like the *Bright Bias* sheath dress on page 68 and the *Patchwork Plus* tent dress with contrasting bands and facings on page 87. Or combine pattern components for unique styles, such as the *Summer in the City* princess dress with added faux vest on page 101. By devising a method of adding interest right at the outset, before you even start sewing, you'll save yourself the challenge of designing a unique mark of distinction when the garment is completed and you want to wear it right away.

Other construction techniques that can be selected for their decorative effects include pleating as used in the *Polka Dot Pizzazz* princess dress on page 95, piping as in the *Positive Piping* shirtwaist dress on page 111, and tucking as in the *Material Magic* tent dress on page 91. These stitch techniques can be so visually interesting by themselves that a dress needs no other embellishment to make it special. If the pattern you choose is plain and simple, it's easy to alter it to include some fabric manipulation like pleating, tucking, or smocking. Just make sure you plan ahead so you can purchase the extra fabric often required and make the changes to the pattern before you start cutting and sewing.

DESIGN AS YOU GO

Look for ways to create decorative effects during the assembly process. For instance, standard facings can be replaced with contrasting reverse facings, and applied bands can both finish seams and add visual interest, as in the *Batik 'n Buttons* ethnic print tent dress on page 70. Adding decorative effects to parts of a pattern as you sew them, such as collar and cuffs, can create a snazzy fashion look you'll never see anywhere else—certainly not in the ready-to-wear departments of the world. Machine embroidery, machine thread lace, pieced fabric, silk ribbon embroidery, and fabric printing or painting are just some of the techniques you can use during garment construction to add flourish to the finished piece.

It's wise to do as much decorative work as possible while the pattern is still in flat pieces. Here again, preplanning is extremely valuable, so you know in advance what you've

got to do to the individual components before sewing them together. For instance, if you're adding a beadwork design to the front bodice of a dress, you will want to complete the beading before the bodice pieces are stitched to the skirt and sleeves, and perhaps even before the bodice pattern is cut out of the fashion fabric. For one thing, it's easier to work with small, flat pieces than with an entire dress, which can be unwieldy and hard to control. Another reason is that the beadwork design is more likely to be accurate and symmetrical when executed on a flat piece of fabric than on one that is curved and contoured by the shaping of the assembled garment style.

APPLIED TRIMS AND GARNISHES

The smallest details can add big-time flair to the simplest of fashions. Braids, ribbons, decorative trims, tapes, laces, and sequins are just a few of the dizzying array of plain and fancy garnishes you can incorporate during sewing or add at the end. To spark your imagination, check back through your inspiration files or look through the current fashion magazines for some of the unconventional and eye-catching effects that can be created with applied details. Don't ever banish a ho-hum garment to the back of your closet without first considering how you can spiff it up with a bit of soutache cord or middy braid, an embroidered patch, a sprinkling of sequins, or several randomly placed single motifs of your sewing machine's prettiest embroidery stitch.

The *Homage to Matisse* tent dress on page 82 illustrates how the designer felt "something else" was needed, and she added some origami-folded parcels of self-fabric in a random pattern around the skirt. Let that "something else" bubble up from your creative depths, and you will surely get lots of

Explore the exciting new territory of buttons for their creative possibilities—a fantastic array of types and styles are out there for you to choose from. Use one type for a dainty feminine effect, another if you want funk and flash.

compliments on your personal design signature.

Buttons used to be merely functional items, purchased to blend in with and even disappear against the fabric of a garment. Luckily for all sewers, however, there's a brave new world of buttons today—thousands of beautiful, whimsical, sedate, and outrageous types made from every imaginable material. Selecting buttons has become one of the most exciting, and most challenging, steps of garment design and creation. In fact, the most difficult part of button-shopping is finally settling on just the right ones. But there couldn't be an easier way of adding uncommon flair to a garment, from delicate freshwater pearl droplet buttons to funky mixed-media mini-sculptures. Because buttons are so easy to change and replace, as the mood strikes or occasion presents itself, you can let yourself go and totally change the look of a garment with a new set of

DESIGNER CAROLYN NORDGREN CARRIES THE THEMES OF HER APPLIQUÉD JUMPER DRESSES TO THE LABELS ON THE INSIDE. SMALL TOUCHES LIKE THESE, EVEN WHEN THEY'RE SIMPLE AND QUICK, HELP A GARMENT STAND OUT FROM THE CROWD AND MAKE A UNIQUE STATEMENT.

buttons. Be creative! There is no law that mandates buttons as closures; they can have a purely decorative purpose, too. Sew them on in a visually interesting design motif, and use invisible notions such as snaps or hooks to perform the basic function of closing the front opening or the cuffs.

ACCESSORIZE FOR CHANGING EFFECTS

Rarely do we ever get dressed without adding a piece of jewelry, scarf, or some other accessory that accents the outfit and pulls it all together. Accessories are a basic building block of every wardrobe, available at a moment's notice to mix with finished outfits in conservative or surprising ways. To get the most mileage out of accessories, keep your current stash in mind as you purchase patterns and fabrics for new sewing projects. If you've got a special piece of jewelry at home, think about how it will look with the pattern and fabric you're considering. For example, a dramatic neckpiece will look gorgeous against a plain jewel-neck bodice; a deep scoop neckline would not set it off as well. A streamlined style in a classy plain fabric can also be a dramatic background to

that embroidered vest or art-to-wear belt back home.

Detachable collars can function as changing accessories for a core group of garments, and they do double duty as showcases for your artistic talents. See the wardrobe of detachable collars on pages 51-55; they greatly expand the fashion versatility of the three basic dresses they mix and match with. Plus, they show off the designer's embroidery artwork. Add a couple of different belts, and you've got an entire spectrum of different looks. Collars can also be the focal point of any garment, as those pictured above demonstrate. The designer has transformed these basic elements into artful objects of beauty in their own right. With such beautiful assemblages of fabric and trim framing the face, no other accessories are needed.

The designers of many of this book's dresses didn't leave accessories to chance. Right from the beginning, they imag-

A Stitch in Time

Topstitching can be an easy finishing touch and attractive way to set off the lines of a garment. Use contrasting thread for a very decorative look or matching thread for a subtle relief effect.

Accessories can be the crowning glory of your original garments, whether purchased or custom made. You don't have to shop all day for the perfect belt; use some leftover fabric scraps to piece together an unusual creation that coordinates perfectly—and is truly unique.

...ined how to coordinate a singular finishing touch with the basic garment. In the *Seersucker Rainbow* shirtwaist dress on page 108, the designer attached free-form fabric tubes and a button-sculpture brooch for unique fashion styling. The designer of the *Woodland Flowers* sheath dress on page 66 and the *Floral Delights* surplice dress on page 128 incorporated self-fabric "epaulets" around the neckline to anchor assorted scarves and fabric swags. For the *Classic Elegance* sheath dress on page 64, the designer made a detachable ascot with covered buttons that can be alternated with an accessorizing shawl or dramatic belt. The *Bright Bias* sheath dress on page 68 has a coordinating slouchy hat made out of

ABOVE, HEMSTITCHED DETACHABLE COLLAR AND FLORAL EMBROIDERED COLLAR

fabric scraps, and the *Sweet Repeats* shirtwaist on page 114 features a simple custom-made embroidered belt that is the perfect accompaniment to the rest of the garment.

Whether the finishing touches of your garments are planned well in advance of construction or conjured up at the very end, they make your custom fashions truly original. The way you put together separate accessories or dovetail design techniques with the assembly process expresses the unique flair of your individual creativity.

ABOVE, CUTWORK COLLAR AND FAUX BRAID COLLAR

A wardrobe of detachable collars like those shown here helps you get a lot of mileage out of a few coordinating dresses. Plus, collars are perfect for experimenting with new techniques and showing off your expert sewing talents.

A WARDROBE OF *Detachable Collars*
DESIGNER: *Mary S. Parker*

Create an entire mix-and-match wardrobe of your favorite dress styles with detachable collars, and then change them according to the occasion or your mood. An added bonus—you can show off your embroidery artwork.

Designer comments

"You spend so much time on a collar, it seems a shame to wear it with only one dress. Making separate collars gives me the opportunity to experiment with different techniques and helps me get a lot of mileage out of the limited time I have to sew."

Materials and supplies

- Dress pattern with V-neck or favorite collar style
- Dress or blouse pattern with favorite collar style, for V-neck dress pattern above
- Fabric of choice for dress
- Approximately ½ yard (.5 m) fabric for each collar
- Approximately ½ yard (.5 m) fusible interfacing for each collar
- Hook-and-loop tape

Materials and tools for collars

Hemstitched collar: wing needle, iron-on temporary stabilizer
Floral embroidered collar: silk-finish cotton or rayon thread, embroidery hoop, tear-away stabilizer
Faux braid collar: silk-finish cotton or rayon thread
Bias strip appliqué collar: approximately ½ yard (.5 m) coordinating fabric, bias tape maker (optional)
Passementerie collar: quilting design template, air-erasable marker, middy braid or soutache cord
Pleated collar: pleater (optional), piping for outside edge
Cutwork collar: silk-finish cotton or rayon thread, iron-on temporary stabilizer, small embroidery scissors to trim fabric away from design

Construction details

1. Make dress according to pattern instructions.

2. To create the detachable collar for a dress pattern with favorite collar style, use the same collar and facing pieces again. To create the detachable collar for a collarless V-neck dress pattern, use the collar, back neck facing, and front facing pieces from a selected dress or blouse pattern.

NOTE: In some patterns, the collar and upper portion of the front facing are a single piece. (This is true for the wing collar of the dresses shown.) If this is the case for the pattern you are using, simply ignore references to the separate front facing in the following instructions.

3. For all versions except the cutwork collar, cut and assemble collar according to pattern instructions, with two exceptions:

a) instead of attaching the under collar to the back neckline of the dress, you will attach it to a separate back neck facing. You will, therefore, cut out a second back neck facing piece.

b) instead of attaching the under collar to the front neckline and opening of the dress, you will attach it to separate shortened front neck facing pieces. You will, therefore, cut out a second set of front neck facing pieces that have been shortened to about 3" (7.5 cm) below where the front edges of the dress overlap.

4. For the pleated collar, pleat enough fabric to cut the upper collar before proceeding with the steps below. Cut the back/neck facings and under collar from unpleated fabric.

5. For all collar versions except the cutwork, apply fusible tricot interfacing to the wrong sides of the upper collar, one of the back neck facing pieces, and two of the shortened front facing pieces.

6. Perform the selected decorative technique to the inter-faced upper collar before joining it to the back neck facing and front facing, if applicable. See specific how-to tips below for the different collar styles.

7. Recommended seam allowances vary according to whether the dress already has a permanently attached collar, such as the wing collar. If the detachable collar will be worn over a permanently attached collar made from the same pattern, construct the detachable collar with ⅜" (1 cm) seam allowances; the detachable collar will then be large enough to fit over and hide the attached collar of the dress. If the detachable collar will be worn with a collarless V-neck dress, use ⅝" (1.5 cm) seam allowances in construction.

8. Join the embellished upper collar to one of the back neck facings and to the first set of front facings (if these are used in your pattern). For the cutwork collar, this completes the construction; finish the seams so they will not ravel.

9. For collars other than the cutwork version, join the under collar to the other back neck facing and the remaining front facings (if these are used in your pattern).

10. Stitch the upper and under collars together along the outside edges in a ⅜" (1 cm) seam. Trim, turn, and press.

11. Use hook-and-loop tape to hold detachable collar in place around the dress neckline, as follows. Cut the tape into squares. Apply a loop-sided (soft) square to the inside of the dress neckline at center back; apply a hook-sided (hard) square to the back facing of the detachable under collar at center back. Apply additional sets of squares at the shoulder seams, taking care that the detachable collar will line up smoothly along the dress neckline and front opening.

12. Mark the front facings of the detachable collar for buttonhole placement, so the collar will be sandwiched between the right and left dress fronts when buttoned. Make buttonholes and cut open.

Hemstitched collar shown on page 51:

The design is formed by sewing with a wing needle, which has "wings" or flanges on either side that cut the fabric as the needle sews, forming a decorative pattern. Experiment with your sewing machine's different zigzag stitches to find an attractive pattern. You may need to reduce the stitch width slightly, to accommodate the needle's wings. Take care to sew an even distance from the edge, using a guide if necessary. Pivot at the collar point. An iron-on, tear-away interfacing will reinforce the fabric while completing the hem-stitching.

DETACHABLE COLLARS, LIKE
THE PASSEMENTERIE VER-
SION AT LEFT AND THE BIAS
STRIP APPLIQUÉ VERSION AT
RIGHT, CAN BE WORN
WITH ANY OF THE THREE
COORDINATING DRESSES.
THE PLEATED VERSION
(INSET) ADDS YET ANOTHER
DIMENSION TO THE CRE-
ATIVE POSSIBILITIES OF THE
COLLARS.

Floral embroidery shown on page 51:

Use a machine-programmed design or hand embroidery to create an attractive design on each collar point. Plan the design to be symmetrical and centered on each collar point. You may want to use an embroidery hoop and tear-away stabilizer.

Faux braid, shown on page 51:

To mimic the look of applied braid, use silk-finish cotton or decorative rayon thread with the widest satin stitch available on your sewing machine. (You will never again search for a braid that matches your outfit!) Take care to sew an even distance from the edge, using a guide if necessary. Pivot at the collar point.

Bias strip appliqué, shown on page 53 and this page

Make a bias strip from coordinating fabric and turn the edges under (a tool for making your own bias strips is a great help with this). Pin the bias strip into place on the upper collar, measuring to make sure it is evenly spaced from the collar edge. Hand-stitch the corners so they look mitered.

Passementerie design, shown on page 52 and this page:

Use a quilting template and air-erasable marker to indicate placement of the soutache cord or middy braid. Couch the cord or braid over the marked design with a narrow zigzag stitch.

Pleated, shown on page 54:

Cut the upper collar from the pleated fabric and apply piping around the collar's outer edges.

Cutwork, shown on page 51:

Use a quilting template to mark a stitch pattern suitable for cutwork treatment or use a suitable machine-programmed design. Reinforce the fabric with an iron-on, tear-away stabilizer. Sew a satin-stitched scalloped edge 3/8" (1 cm) from the edge of the collar. Satin stitch the pattern, following the design markings, and trim away the fabric close to the stitching.

Tips from the designer

■ If you are using a pattern for a different garment to create the detachable collar, check to see how it will go with the dress you intend to wear it with. Insert the other garment, which has the desired collar style, inside the dress. Check that the low point of the dress V-neck is low enough so that the selected collar will fasten at the intended point. Check also that the V-neck is not so low that the collar will be too small to fill up the neck area.

■ When using an air-erasable marker to trace a design, don't forget to test it first on a scrap of the fashion fabric to be sure it will disappear completely.

Despite the best-laid plans and all the care in the world, tragedy can strike in the sewing room. You can carefully review every construction step before you start and painstakingly stitch the garment together only to find out when it's too late that somewhere along the line, something went wrong. Perhaps the fabric had a slight nap after all, and the left and right fronts are ever so slightly different in color. Or you forgot to turn the pattern piece over to cut a mirror-image piece and now you have two right fronts, but no left. Maybe you shortened the upper sleeve to fit your arm, but forgot to do the same to the under sleeve. Or somehow, late at night, you managed to put the zipper in upside down or inside out.

Don't feel all alone—these mishaps happen to everyone; they always have, and always will. In fact, some of these learning experiences seem to repeat themselves periodically even though we swear we'll never have to learn those lessons again! But we do relearn them over and over, and still we keep on sewing.

WHEN THE ALARM GOES OFF

When you discover a problem or error and the "emergency" alarm starts ringing in your brain, **stop** what you are doing right away. When your heart starts to race because you suspect something is wrong, or your shears slice right through a finished seam and there can be no doubt that something is wrong, cease and desist. Stop cutting or sewing, get up from what you're doing, and leave the area—just like a fire drill.

A Stitch in Time

If laundering the finished garment turns up some unforeseen problems, wear an attractive overblouse, vest, or jacket to cover them up—no one will be the wiser. Just remember to pretreat all fabrics and interfacings next time!

A Stitch in Time

The "rip and redo" method of correcting errors is time-tested and proven to get good results. Just settle down with your seam ripper, a cold drink, and some good music to make the rehab work go fast.

This gives you a chance to calm down and get away from the problem. It will also prevent you from slicing your garment-in-progress to shreds and tossing it in the wastebasket in a frustrated rage—although, at times, this can be a very therapeutic thing to do. Stay away from the sewing area for at least an hour, and preferably overnight. When you come back to it, the frustration will have dissipated and you'll be able to more reasonably assess the damage and devise a solution.

CUTTING ERRORS

Mishaps at the cutting table are the easiest to remedy because they happen so early in the sewing process. If you have enough extra fabric, simply recut and enjoy a sigh of relief. If not, a trip to your local fabric shop may yield the replacement yardage you need. However, if the material is out of stock when you return to buy, you're faced with a greater challenge. This is when those old sayings about necessity being the mother of invention and problems being opportunities come in handy!

As soon as you can stand to look at it, take stock of the extent of the damage. If you made just a small error in cutting, perhaps you can hide it in the seam allowance or repair it with a fusible web product. If the mistaken cut is more significant, take a look at the overall pattern and try to figure out how to accommodate the problem. Can you shorten the afflicted piece—long sleeves to short, short sleeves to cap, ankle length to knee? Or can you recut the piece out of contrasting fabric—white linen collar on the original pearl grey linen coat dress? If you decide to make the contrast obvious, consider replacing some other garment components as well, even if they were cut out without incident. For example, if you have to replace the collar, go for a new set of cuffs, too, and maybe even the back yoke. If a skirt piece was the casualty, think about splitting the pattern pieces and doing some subtle or bright fabric piecing combinations—for example, left front/back right in one color and right front/back left in another or a whole new skirt pieced from several fabrics. If a bodice piece was the victim, mend the error and cover the problem with a faux vest; the *Summer in the City* dress on page 101 demonstrates how stylish such a vest can be, but it can also be a great camouflage device. Whichever creative fix you come up with, the result should look as if you planned it from the very beginning. No one ever has to know that your ingenuity was really damage control, unless you tell them—so don't!

If your scissors take a wrong turn during the assembly process and a cutting mishap occurs, choke back your tears and experiment with your sewing machine's mending capabilities. You can often repair it so it won't show; if not, then mend it with a decorative stitch motif that will look like an appliqué. However, make sure you repeat the same

appliqué illusion at several different places on the garment so the single "fix-it" motif doesn't look so obvious. Alternatively, make some appliqué motifs out of coordinating fabric and attach them to the problem spot and other areas of the garment. If the accidental slash is major, your dress may have to become a blouse or the long-sleeved style may have to be sleeveless. As long as you can still wear the completed garment and no one knows what it was originally meant to be, you have no reason to grieve.

STITCHING ERRORS

The preferred way to make amends for stitching blunders is to take out the stitches and repeat the construction step. Granted, this is never fun, but with a seam ripper in hand

and some good music to listen to, you can complete the "rip and redo" step quickly and painlessly. Basting complex seams before you stitch can save you from this type of disaster because you can check the seam from the right side before it's permanently installed. This extra basting step is definitely worth the time, to guarantee that sleeves are stitched correctly into the right armholes and that curved princess seams are smooth and unpuckered.

If you trimmed a seam too close after stitching it and it starts to unravel, get out the fray retardant and apply a healing drop. If the stitching is just messy and imperfect, but not wrong, it's easy to disguise with decorative stitching on top, applied contrast bands or ornamental trim, or with some well-placed dramatic accessories.

FITTING PROBLEMS

Before you begin sewing, you should have either made a muslin or tested the fit of the pattern. During construction, you should retest the fit regularly. However, if the finished garment still doesn't fit right or you just don't like the way the fit looks, consider some remedial efforts before you give up. If

A Stitch in Time

Don't waste time or creative energy mourning your disasters. Recycle what you can, cut up the fabric and quilt it, or toss the finished item in the trash—this can be surprisingly therapeutic.

there is still some leeway in the seam allowances, you can open the seams and take them in or let them out. If the fit is too tight in places, consider slashing the garment and adding gussets or gores, to increase comfort ease or add width. Shoulder pads can often fix a poorly fitting shoulder/neckline area, and an unflattering overall look may be surprisingly improved just by raising or lowering the hemline a bit. If you finally decide that the fit won't ever look right or be comfortable to wear, take the garment apart and use the well-fitting components in a new project.

A Stitch in Time

As soon as you detect an error, stop what you're doing and leave the area, just like a fire drill. Take a break and let the panic or frustration subside. When you come back to the disaster later, or tomorrow, you'll be able to figure out what to do calmly.

POST-CONSTRUCTION AILMENTS

Your new garment may be absolutely perfect in every way, until after its first laundering or cleaning, when some kind of sewing monster rears its ugly head. Most of these ailments are due to incomplete or haphazard pretreating. All interfacings and notions, as well as the fashion fabric, should be pretreated so they don't act up after a wash-and-dry session. For example, a fusible interfacing may shrink more than the fashion fabric, causing unsightly bubbling and puckering. In these cases, there's not much you can do except cover the flaws with a jacket or vest and promise that you will preshrink everything in the future. Colors that run, fade, or bleed might not be too obvious to the casual observer, and the effect might mellow with repeated laundering. Again, pretreating the fabric and setting questionable colors with a diluted vinegar/water solution can prevent future occurrences. If the color blemish is restricted to a small area, an embroidered embellishment or appliqué patch will cover it up.

Correcting errors and saving disasters might be a good skill-building technique, but a better strategy is to be attentive throughout the sewing preparation steps and every stage of

A Stitch in Time

If you don't have enough leftover fabric to cover a cutting mishap, and the fabric store is sold out, cover the problem with a decorative appliqué or cut some pattern pieces (e.g. collar and cuffs, or front and back yokes) out of contrast fabric—for an intentional-looking result.

construction. Review every single "next step" one more time before you start cutting or stitching—it takes just a few seconds, but can save hours of agony and loads of money.

If a sewing catastrophe occurs in spite of your best intentions, go easy on yourself. Try your best to solve the problem. If the situation cannot be fixed, no matter what you do, don't waste any more time and creative energy worrying over it. Recycle as much as you can from the garment and toss the rest. Cut off and save the buttons, stash unseamed areas of fabric for future bias binding, use pieces of the fabric in a patchwork project, or stuff pillows with it. Discard whatever is left over or non-recyclable, and chalk the disaster up to experience—there's always room for more of that.

A Stitch in Time

Design a faux cover-up to hide an error. An attached vest can camouflage a problem bodice and a skirt overlay can make a mending job invisible. Both fix-its will look like the creative interpretation of a pattern instead of damage control.

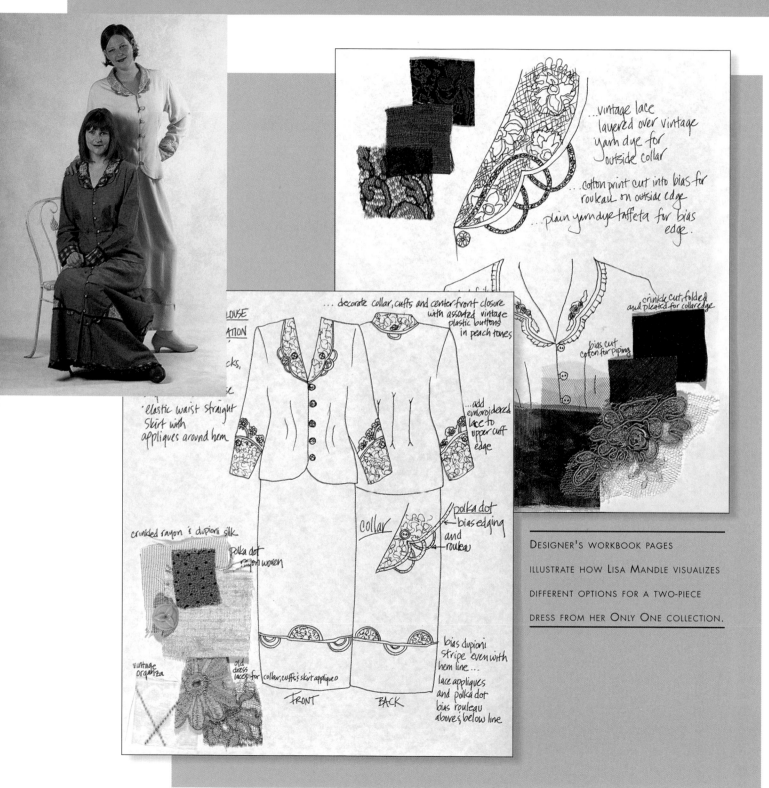

...vintage lace layered over vintage yarn dye for outside collar

...cotton print cut into bias for rouleau on outside edge

...plain yarn dye taffeta for bias edge.

...decorate collar, cuffs and center front closure with assorted vintage plastic buttons in peach tones

...add embroidered lace to upper cuff edge

crinkle cut folded and pleated for collar edge

bias cut cotton for piping

LOUSE
ATION

cks,

se

elastic waist straight skirt with appliques around hem

polka dot bias edging and rouleau

collar

crinkled rayon & dupioni silk

Polka dot rayon woven

vintage organza

old dress laces for collar, cuffs & skirt applique

FRONT   BACK

bias dupioni stripe even with hem line...
lace appliques and polka dot bias rouleau above & below line

DESIGNER'S WORKBOOK PAGES
ILLUSTRATE HOW LISA MANDLE VISUALIZES
DIFFERENT OPTIONS FOR A TWO-PIECE
DRESS FROM HER ONLY ONE COLLECTION.

get ready, get set...sew!

The dresses featured in this final section all started with a simple, basic concept. Regardless of how fancy or ornate the finished garments appear, inside every one of them is the silhouette of a classic style made from a standard pattern. Yet the variety of the results proves that what makes a dress truly special is the individual imprint of the sewer's creative inspiration. A simple dress style can be a foundation for decorative stitching, a backdrop for some lace accents, or a setting for dramatic color blocking. The underlying dress styles may be the same, but their final effects are excitingly diverse. The sewers who made the dresses in these pages share with you step-by-step the embellishments they added or techniques they used to transform their old standby patterns into brand new wearables. You will recognize the standard styles, no doubt, and will surely be inspired with ideas of your own for giving your favorite dress patterns a new creative life.

DIFFERENT COLOR SCHEMES AND FABRICS, AS WELL AS A FULLER-CUT SKIRT IN THE VERSION BELOW, VARY THE SAME BASIC STYLE FOR DAYTIME AND EVENING.

THE DRESS STYLES

SHIRTWAIST

The shirtwaist dress is a classic style that seems to come back into fashion at regular intervals. When it's "out," you can't find one, but when it's "in," the shirtwaist always looks fresh and up-to-date, with short or long sleeves, straight or full skirts. Shirtwaist enthusiasts sew them regardless of the fashion world's forecasts and wear them all their lives.

While variations on a theme can be nearly infinite, the number of themes in the world of dress fashion is pretty limited. Designers and sewers keep coming back to the basic styles because they are familiar, easy to fit, simple to sew, and predictable in their flattering results. The designers for this volume used several of these classic dress silhouettes as starting points for their creative interpretation: the sheath, tent dress or "big" dress, princess seam dress, shirtwaist, coat dress, and other styles such as dropped waist, surplice or wrap, and raised or empire waist.

TENT DRESS

The tent dress, also referred to as the big dress, is a casual and loose-fitting style that women love to wear because it is so comfortable. It can be a pullover jumper model or a buttoned front dress version, and may or may not include several other style details. For example, it may be sleeveless or short-sleeved and it may or may not have a collar and waist seam.

SHEATH

The sheath dress is a no-waist style also referred to as a chemise. It is usually straight, but can also be somewhat A-line, and is probably the most classically simple style there is. A sheath requires little yardage, making it a modest investment in fabric, and is very quick to make. Its spare, simple shape makes it a perfect wardrobe building block, paired with vests, jackets, overblouses, or assorted accessories.

COAT DRESS

The coat dress is elegant, businesslike, and classy. Whether single-breasted or double-breasted, this front-closing style is usually quite tailored. Its collars and cuffs lend themselves to creative interpretation with contrasting fabrics and decorative stitching, and the buttoned front closing is a natural showcase for unique buttons.

PRINCESS SEAM DRESS

The princess style dress is a classically beautiful style, probably because it is flattering to most figures and is easy to customize the fit for individual shapes. Its curved seams can emerge from the armhole or the shoulder seam, and the skirt can be flared or straight. This type of dress is very versatile, appropriate for conservative, professional styles as well as feminine looks, including most bridal fashions.

OTHER DRESS STYLES

Other common dresses include the wrap-front or surplice, the raised empire waist, and the dropped waist. All of these traditional styles are featured in the following pages, updated for today with some very untraditional innovations.

Classic Elegance
DESIGNER:
Marion E. Mathews

This classic style has a slimming effect, which is accentuated with a vertical band of Ultrasuede. A detachable ascot with covered buttons is just one of several possible accessories that make this dress so versatile.

Designer comments

"To showcase the fabric, I decided to keep the lines of the dress straight and simple. Then I can change the overall look with a shawl, scarf, belt, or the Ultrasuede ascot."

Materials and supplies

- Pattern for no-waist dress with front opening
- Fabric of choice
- ¼ yard (.25 m) Ultrasuede
- Covered button kit
- Zipper for back opening

Pattern and design changes

1. The designer started with a straight dress that buttoned up the front. Because she prefers back closures, she made a zipper opening in the back. This saved the time spent on buttonholes and also eliminated any alterations required by possible gapping at the front opening.

2. She replaced the front opening with a vertical band of Ultrasuede, and added matching bands at the sleeve ends. She saved a bit of Ultrasuede to make a detachable ascot and used fabric scraps to make covered buttons for the ascot.

3. She added width to make the skirt a bit more A-line, by graduating the side cutting lines to the largest size of a multi-size pattern. See Figure 1.

Construction details:

1. Cut the band collar and interfacing on the bias, for greater flexibility at the back opening.

PLAN FOR THE WEEK

Monday:

❧ ~ ~ ❧

Tuesday:

❧ ~ ~ ❧

Wednesday:

❧ ~ ~ ❧

Thursday:
Pretreat fabric.

Friday:
Make pattern alterations; cut out dress, mark, and interface appropriate pieces.

Saturday:
Begin dress assembly; cut and apply Ultrasuede bands; hem sleeves.

Sunday:
Complete assembly; hem; make ascot and covered buttons.

2. When topstitching bands in place, go slowly or use a guide, to be sure the lines of stitching are straight and parallel to the edges of the bands.

Tips from the designer

■ For a matte finish to the bands, let the reverse side of the Ultrasuede show.

■ Check sleeve length as soon as possible, so you can make adjustments, if needed. You can compare your arm measurement with the length of the sleeve pattern piece, try on the pattern tissue, or try on the finished sleeve before hemming and inserting into the dress.

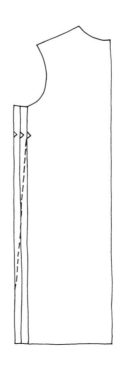

Fig. 1.
If you use a multi-size pattern, draw a new cutting line from your size to a larger size, to make a straight skirt more A-line. Or use the various lines of the different sizes to accommodate the measurements of your unique figure.

Woodland Flowers
DESIGNER:
Sheila Bennitt

A simple T-shirt tunic is lengthened and widened to become a fun loose-fitting dress. Contrasting pink rolled hem edges brighten up this spring-like fashion.

Designer comments

"I love layering garments for a creative look. This piece could be a dress worn over tights or a tunic worn over slim pants. Either way, it's colorful and interesting."

Materials and supplies

- Pattern for T-shirt tunic
- Fabric of choice
- Woolly nylon thread
- Tools
- Serger
- Embroidery foot or rolled hem attachment

Pattern and design changes

1. The designer started with a basic T-shirt tunic pattern, adding width and length to the body.

2. She then created two angled tucks, at the right waist and right hip, for a nicely draped effect.

3. She lengthened the sleeves by adding two self-fabric bands stitched together in the pink accent thread.

4. She also added self-fabric belt ends to the back, to draw in the overall silhouette a bit when tied.

5. She attached epaulet loops at the shoulder, center front, and center back, so that a self-fabric scarf can be threaded through and draped around the neck in different ways.

Tips from the designer

- Think about using the rolled hem edges as design elements. You can split any pattern piece, add a bit of seam allowance, and then sew the pieces together with a contrasting and colorful thread. It creates a nice graphic effect, especially on a printed fabric.

Plan for the week

Monday:

Tuesday:

Wednesday:

Thursday:
Pretreat fabric.

Friday:
Cut out dress; make tucks in right front.

Saturday:
Assemble dress.

Sunday:
Make self-fabric scarf; make and attach epaulets.

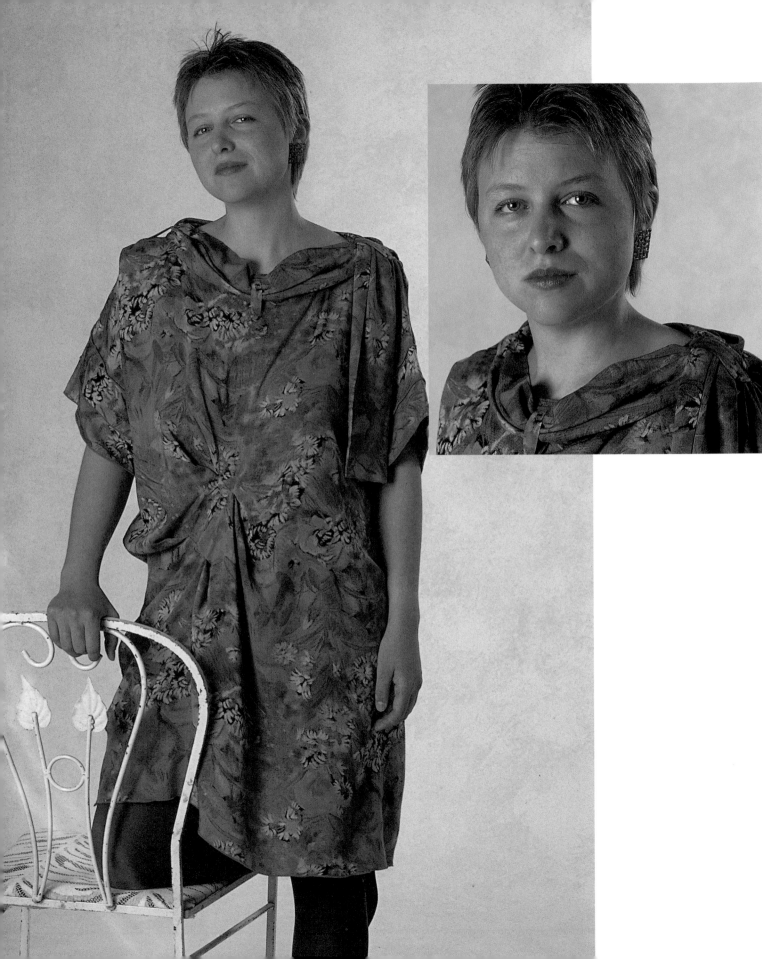

Bright Bias

DESIGNER:

Joyce Baldwin

Arranging striped fabric to create geometric patterns is easy and has nearly infinite possibilities. Big bold stripes will give a completely different effect than delicate pastel pinstripes. Experiment for lots of options.

Designer comments

"This dress was inspired by a photograph from my clip files and a piece of fabric. Sufficient scraps were left over after making the dress to create a matching hat with ribbon cockade."

Materials and supplies

- Pattern for no-waist A-line sheath or jumper

- Striped fabric of choice

NOTE: Directional stripes and large-scale patterns usually require more fabric, to ensure matching at seams.

Pattern and design changes

The designer started with an older pattern for a no-waist flared dress with sleeves. For the stripe arrangement, she slashed the pattern horizontally and vertically to create the seams. See Figure 1. She also reduced the flare for more of an A-line effect, added a bit of wearing ease, and created armhole facings. See Figure 2. Before cutting the fashion fabric, she made a sample garment of inexpensive striped fabric to test the fit and the positioning of the stripes.

Construction details

NOTE: See Figures 1 and 2 for numbered construction details listed below.

1. Replace center front foldline with seam allowances, to create seam for stripe placement.

2. Remove hem flare at center back by making seam parallel to grainline.

3. Remove approximately 4½" (11.5 cm) of hem flare at front and back side seams.

4. Increase front and back side seams ¼" (6 mm) for a total

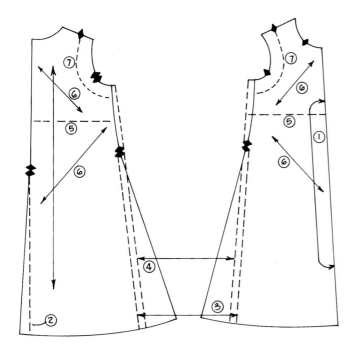

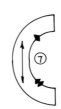

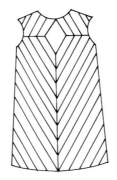

Fig. 1.
Update an older pattern to add ease for today's preferred wearing comfort, and slash pieces to accommodate creative stripe arrangements. See "Construction details."

Fig. 2.
Draft separate armhole facings for dress front and back.

Fig. 3.
Many design options are possible with stripe arrangements, including this variation that raises the horizontal seam and creates an interesting opening.

increase of 1" (2.5 cm), to loosen overall fit and compensate for reduced hem flare.

5. Slash front and back approximately 1½" (4 cm) above waistline and add seam allowances to both slashed edges.

6. Establish true bias grainlines.

7. Draft separate armhole facings; overlap stitching lines at shoulder and draw grainline. See Figure 2.

Tips from the designer

■ The horizontal seam must be at a right angle to the vertical center front and center back seams. If it is not, the angle of stripes will not match exactly where they meet at the horizontal seam.

■ Experiment with different stripe arrangements before cutting and sewing the fashion fabric.

■ The same stripe pattern used in the dress shown here could be modified by moving the horizontal seam up and making a faced opening at the intersection of the horizontal and vertical seams. This would create a diamond-shaped opening. See Figure 3.

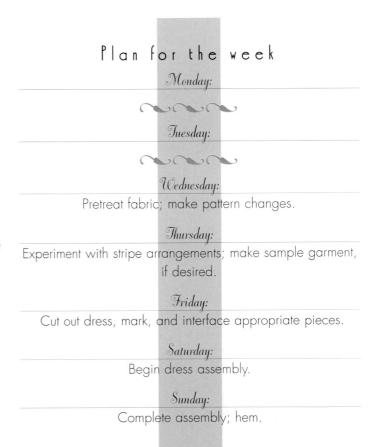

Plan for the week

Monday:

Tuesday:

Wednesday:
Pretreat fabric; make pattern changes.

Thursday:
Experiment with stripe arrangements; make sample garment, if desired.

Friday:
Cut out dress, mark, and interface appropriate pieces.

Saturday:
Begin dress assembly.

Sunday:
Complete assembly; hem.

Batik 'n Buttons

DESIGNER:
M. Luanne Carson

Whip up this comfortable tent dress quickly from a favorite pattern, then make it special. It's easy with a few unique buttons, some contrast bands, and several "prairie point" accents made from remnants in your leftovers box.

Designer comments

"I raided my fabric stash for small amounts of coordinating prints to go with the ethnic designs of the bodice and skirt. The five buttons were 'uglies' I found in a grab bag, but they became beautiful when put together with this combination of fabrics."

Materials and supplies

■ Tent or "big" dress pattern

■ Assorted coordinating or contrasting fabrics of choice

■ Decorative buttons

Construction details

1. Stitch various bands of coordinating or contrasting fabrics together before cutting out skirt pieces. It may take some time to come up with an arrangement that is both attractive and the right proportions for the dress—you might want to experiment first on samples.

2. Assemble dress.

3. Make several prairie points out of coordinating or contrasting fabrics. See Figure 1.

4. Stitch prairie points into the seams when contrast bands are first constructed or stitch them in place later along the bands wherever you think something else is needed for visual effect, using a satin stitch or narrow zigzag.

5. Topstitch decorative strip along center of lower contrast band.

6. Attach buttons in random order along lower contrast band.

Tips from the designer

■ The bottom-most band of the skirt is actually a double thickness of fabric, to provide weight and eliminate the need for a hem.

Plan for the week

Monday:

Tuesday:

Wednesday:

Thursday:

Friday:
Pretreat fabric; experiment with bands of coordinating fabrics for skirt.

Saturday:
Construct skirt fabric from coordinating bands; cut out dress, mark, and interface appropriate pieces; begin dress assembly.

Sunday:
Complete assembly; make and attach prairie points and decorative strip; sew on buttons.

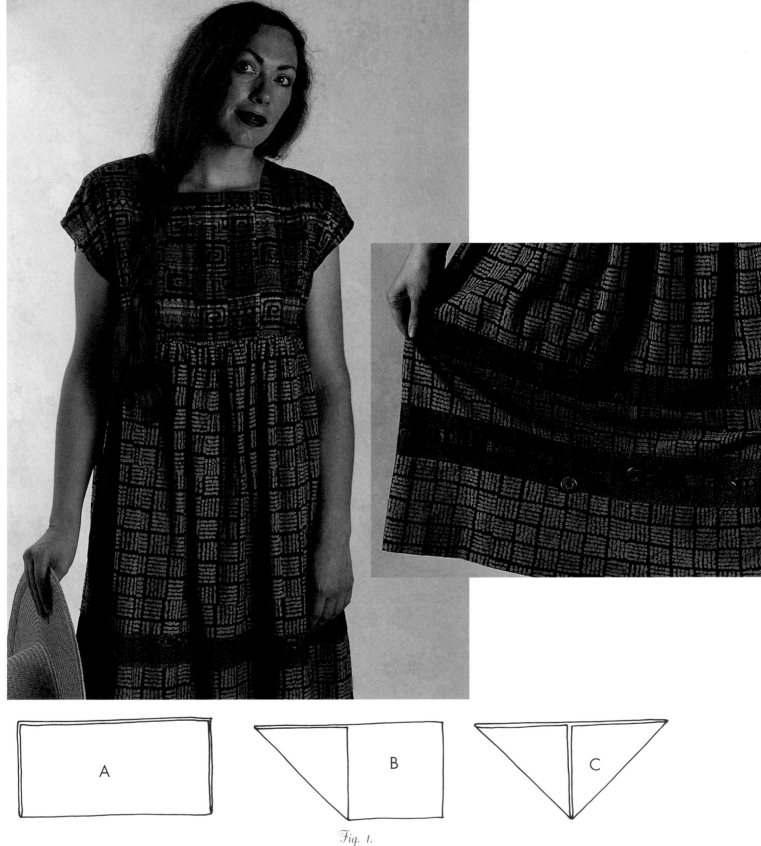

Fig. 1.

To make a prairie point, fold a fabric square in half (A), turn one folded corner up to opposite raw edge (B), and then the other (C) to form a triangle or "point." Stitch raw edge of prairie point into a seam.

Mammy's Garden
DESIGNER:
Karen M. Bennett

If you love to garden, here's a beautiful way to create bouquets of flowers during the off season when you can't be outside, working in the flower beds.

Designer comments

"Mammy's Garden is named for my grandmother, who taught me to tat. She learned when she was five years old and tatted for the vast majority of her 95 years. Her legacy includes bridal garters, snowflakes, and miles of edgings. I will always thank Mammy for the love of fine handwork she instilled in me, and I'm teaching my three daughters to tat in order to pass on the family heritage."

Materials and supplies

- Pattern for tent or "big" dress with buttoned front opening
- Fabric of choice, including extra for bodice lining and covered buttons
- Covered button kit for 13 buttons

For silk ribbon embroidery:

- 2 mm silk ribbon for background stem
- 4 mm silk ribbon for leaves and flowers
- Glass beads for accents
- Quilting thread to sew beads to fabric

For tatting:

- Size 12 pearl cotton for tatted flowers

Tools

- Chenille needles for silk ribbon embroidery
- Embroidery hoop
- Beading needle
- Milliner's needle, size 8, for sewing beads to fabric
- Tatting shuttle

Pattern and design changes

1. The designer added waist darts to the front and back bodice for a more fitted look. In the back, darts are 6" (15 cm) long, 1⅜" (3.5 cm) wide at the dart base, and placed 4" (10 cm) in from center back to center of dart. In the front, darts are 5⅜" (13.75 cm) long, 1⅛" (2.75 cm) wide at the dart base, and 5¼" (13.5 cm) in from front edge.

2. She replaced the 2¼" (5.5 cm) front opening facing with a ⅝" (1.5 cm) seam allowance, in order to line the entire front and back bodice with self-fabric, making sure that the right front opening overlaps the left front for button and buttonhole placement.

Construction details

1. Cut two bodice back pieces; one will be used for lining.

2. Trace outline of right and left front bodice pieces onto larger rectangles of fabric; do not cut bodice pieces out until after completing embroidery. The rectangles of fabric are needed to fit into embroidery hoop. (NOTE: Remember to flip the pattern piece over, to get both a left and right bodice, maintaining front edge overlap on right piece.) See Figure 1.

3. Embroider as desired and accent with beads and tatting. Make sure there's a left and right side to the design.

4. When embroidery is completed, lightly steam back side of fabric before cutting bodice pieces out of fabric rectangles.

5. Assemble bodice.

6. Interface front opening edges of self-fabric bodice lining; assemble bodice lining and attach to bodice.¹

7. Assemble and finish dress.

8. Cover buttons with self-fabric and sew to dress.

Tatted flowers

```
KEY FOR TATTING:

    – = picot

    + = join

    • = bead

   cl = close

    R = ring

number = # of double stitches
```

For three-petal flowers, thread six beads on tatting shuttle for each flower.

R 2 • 2 – • – 2 • 2 cl
R 2 + 2 – • – 2 • 2 cl
R 2 + 2 – • – 2 + 2 cl

For five-petal flowers, thread ten beads on tatting shuttle for each flower.

R 3 • 3 – • – 3 • 3 cl
R 3 + 3 – • – 3 • 3 cl
R 3 + 3 – • – 3 • 3 cl
R 3 + 3 – • – 3 • 3 cl
R 3 + 3 – • – 3 + 3 cl

Tips from the designer

■ Streamline sewing by stitching as many seams as possible, then press and go on to next steps.

■ Jot down notes about the adjustments you make as you go; store your notes with the pattern, for the next time you sew it up.

For more information about silk ribbon embroidery and tatting:
Jones, Rebecca. *The Complete Book of Tatting*. London: Dryad Press Ltd.,1985.
Montano, Judith Baker. *The Art of Silk Ribbon Embroidery*. Lafayette, California: C&T Publishing, 1993.

Plan for the week

Monday:
pretreat fabric.

Tuesday:
Make pattern changes and cut rectangles for bodice pieces; begin silk ribbon embroidery.

Wednesday:
Complete embroidery.

Thursday:
Cut out dress, mark, and interface appropriate pieces; begin tatting.

Friday:
Continue tatting.

Saturday:
Complete tatting; cut out bodice pieces; begin dress assembly.

Sunday:
Complete assembly; cover buttons; hem.

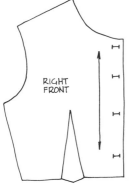

RIGHT
FRONT

SINGLE LAYER OF FABRIC

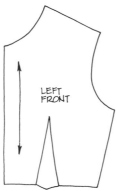

LEFT
FRONT

SINGLE LAYER OF FABRIC

Fig. 1.
Trace right and left bodice pieces onto rectangles of fabric, but don't cut them out until after the embroidery is completed. Don't forget to flip the pattern piece over so you'll have a left and a right. Right front has an added overlap for the buttons.

Garden Party Dress
DESIGNER:
Karen Swing

Create a one-of-a-kind lace collar and then personalize the color by assembling the dress completely and dyeing it, lace and all. You won't have to shop for matching thread and you'll make a perfectly coordinated impression.

Designer comments

"My intent was to take advantage of the various ways different fibers take dye, creating a dress with coordinated shades of the same color. By completing a garment before dyeing it, I never have to buy four spools of the right color for my serger. Even my seam finishes are always perfectly matched."

Materials and supplies

- Tent or "big" dress pattern

- White fabric of choice, plus one yard for shrinkage and for making bias tape

- White cotton thread

- Assorted natural fiber novelty threads—silk, cotton, rayon, etc.

- Heat-soluble stabilizer

- Covered button kit

- Fray retardant

- Dye in color of choice

Pattern and design changes

1. Instead of cutting the upper collar from fabric, the designer created a collar of free-form machine-stitched lace, which was then attached to the under collar and edged with a self-fabric bias binding.

2. She eliminated the pattern's side seam pockets, to prevent sagging at the hips caused by weight (e.g., car keys or other pocket contents).

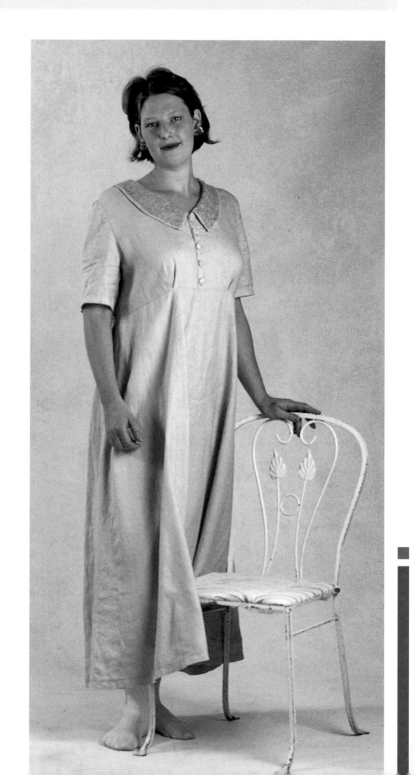

Construction details

To make lace:

1. Trace the full collar pattern onto heat soluble stabilizer with waterproof or disappearing ink pen, adding approximately ½" (1.25 cm) around the entire collar; this extra will be taken up by the stitching for the lace and by the shrinkage of the dye bath.

2. Mark five circles on the stabilizer (use the empty space within the collar's neck edge) for the covered button lace. See Figure 1. A good rule of thumb is to make the circles twice the size of the button.

3. With a novelty thread in the bobbin, stitch the stabilizer in random designs over the collar and button shapes, starting with the thickest thread. Adjust the tension so the thread pulls easily from the bobbin case; check the "feel" of regular thread before you change the tension so you know how it should pull. Bypassing the bobbin case's tension spring entirely gives a wonderful bouclé texture.

4. Repeat with the other novelty threads. Stitch areas slightly larger than the sizes of the collar and button covers, to account for slight shrinkage and so that no raw ends will be visible in the finished lace.

5. Remove stabilizer according the manufacturer's instructions. If you discover gaps in the lace, place a scrap of stabilizer underneath and fill the gap with stitching, starting from the edge of the collar so no raw ends will be visible.

6. Steam the lace to preshrink before cutting out the collar pattern.

To finish collar:

1. Carefully machine baste lace to under collar, randomly following the lines of the lace pattern. You won't have to remove the basting thread, because it will be dyed along with everything else.

2. Press the collar well, with lots of steam; take care not to stretch it out of shape, using the collar pattern as a template.

3. Cut off the ⅝" (1.5 cm) seam allowance along the outside edge of the collar and seal any raw threads with fray retardant.

4. Bind the outside edge with a bias-cut self-fabric strip and press well.

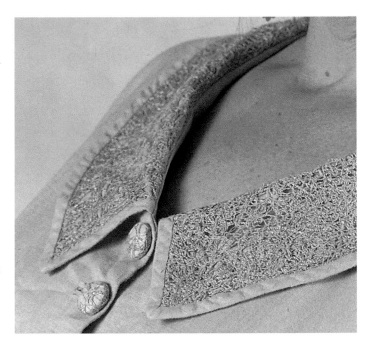

For covered buttons:

1. Cut out five lace circles and five self-fabric circles; lay each lace circle on top of a fabric circle and cover buttons according to manufacturer's instructions.

For dyeing the finished dress:

1. Once the dress is entirely completed, including sewing on the buttons with white thread, dye it according to manufacturer's instructions.

2. If you normally use fray retardant to seal buttonhole threads, dye won't be taken up where you use it. Therefore, don't cut open and seal the buttonholes until after the dress is dyed.

Tips from the designer

■ Consider the method of dyeing you will use, when selecting fabric. For instance, hot water dyes will cause more shrinkage than warm water, so you may need to purchase extra fabric.

■ Remember that once you remove the stabilizer from the lace collar and button covers, there will be nothing holding the lace together. Therefore, be sure to overlap your stitching often so the threads interlink well throughout the piece of lace.

■ Add leftover scraps to the dye bath, in case of emergencies or a change of heart. Once the dress was finished I wished I had included the pattern's ties in the back. But, with no matching fabric, I had no way to add them.

Fig. 1.
Trace the collar pattern and circles for covered buttons onto the stabilizer, and then free-form stitch in a random pattern over all. The button covers should fit in the space inside the collar neckline.

Plan for the week

Monday:

Tuesday:
Pretreat fabric; make pattern alterations, if needed.

Wednesday:
Cut out and mark dress; cut collar pattern from stabilizer; practice machine lace embroidery.

Thursday:
Make collar lace.

Friday:
Begin dress assembly; attach lace to under collar and bind edge.

Saturday:
Complete assembly; make buttonholes; cover buttons and sew to dress; hem.

Sunday:
Dye dress.

Sashiko Style
DESIGNER:
Mary S. Parker

This dress proves that simplicity can make a most elegant statement, turning a basic denim look into something truly special. The Sashiko technique of machine embroidery is used here to make a Cypress Fence pattern, but the design possibilities are nearly infinite.

Designer comments

"I love doing this type of embroidery, and the simple lines of this dress let me work out an entire design without having to worry about seams or darts interfering."

Materials and supplies

- Tent dress or jumper pattern, or sleeveless dress and well-fitting jewel-neck blouse patterns

- Dress-weight fabric of choice, preferably in a dark or bright color that will contrast nicely with the white Sashiko thread

- Iron-on transfer pens

- Totally Stable™ or other non-woven fusible tear-away stabilizer

- Teflon sheet, usually sold to protect ironing board when fusing interfacing onto fashion fabric

- White topstitching weight thread

- White regular weight thread

Pattern and design changes

1. The designer started with a sleeveless dress pattern and merged it with a well-fitting blouse pattern to get the slightly higher neckline and straight sleeves.

2. For a more flattering hang to the garment, she also moved the grainline of the front and back pieces so that it was in the center of the panels rather than along the front or back edge. See Figure 1 on page 116.

for ironing the transfer onto the stabilizer before ironing the stabilizer onto the fabric. You can then iron the stabilizer to the fabric at a lower temperature than if you were transferring the design after the stabilizer was attached to the fabric—making it much easier to tear away later.

1. Cut out the jumper or dress pattern according to manufacturer's instructions.

2. Create a full-size pattern for the central, interlocking part of the Sashiko design on the dress front.

3. Photocopy the design and then trace over the lines with iron-on transfer pens.

4. Place a sheet of stabilizer, shiny side down, on your cutting table. Place dress front pattern piece on top, so that shoulders and neck edges are at the top edge of the stabilizer sheet. Use a pencil to trace the outline of the top area of the dress front pattern. Set pattern aside and cut out the stabilizer along the outline you have marked.

Construction details

The designer used a two-step process for making the iron-on transfer pattern for the Sashiko embroidery. The tear-away stabilizer is easier to remove from the fashion fabric, after completing the embroidery stitching, if you use a Teflon sheet

5. Center the iron-on transfer (ink side down) on top of the stabilizer bodice that you just cut out, and secure with several pins.

6. Place the stabilizer bodice, shiny side down, on top of a Teflon sheet on your ironing board. Remove pins and iron the transfer design to the stabilizer according to manufacturer's directions. Lift the transfer away and set aside. The stabilizer will lift up easily from the Teflon sheet.

7. With shiny side of stabilizer against wrong side of dress front (the transferred design will be facing up), iron lightly to secure. NOTE: You don't want to bond the stabilizer to the fabric permanently because you will have to tear it away later; iron lightly at first and touch up loosened areas if needed.

8. Decide how you wish to extend the embroidered design lines from the bodice center to the outside edges of the dress front. Iron on additional stabilizer in the areas where extended stitching will be. Use a yardstick and pencil to draw the lines to the outer edges.

9. Thread sewing machine bobbin with topstitching weight thread and the needle with regular weight thread. You may have to loosen bobbin tension, as well as tighten needle tension, for a good-looking stitch; experiment on a scrap before sewing on the dress.

10. The Sashiko embroidery will be stitched with the right side of the fashion fabric against the feed dogs of the sewing machine and the iron-on transfer design on top. Sew the design, following the iron-on transfer and the penciled extended lines. To avoid stitching over a loose tail of bobbin thread, always pull the bobbin thread up to the iron-on transfer side (wrong side) of the fabric as soon as you have stitched far enough away that this can be done.

11. When the embroidery stitching is completed, tie off all bobbin threads with their corresponding needle threads in tight double square knots (tie right over left, then left over right). Trim thread tails to about 1" (2.5 cm).

12. Gently tear away the stabilizer.

13. To keep the square knots from loosening in the wash, protect the inside of the dress by ironing a piece of lightweight fusible interfacing over the knotted areas of the design.

14. Assemble the dress, according to pattern instructions.

Tips from the designer

■ The Cypress Fence pattern requires quite a bit of stop-and-start stitching and knot-tying on the wrong side. If you prefer a design that can be sewn continuously, refer to some of the books available on Sashiko embroidery for a myriad of alternatives.

■ If your sewing machine has a "needle down" setting, it will come in handy to keep the fabric from shifting as you pivot the stitching along the design lines. Otherwise, use your hands to hold the fabric securely as you pivot.

Plan for the week

Monday:

Tuesday:

Wednesday:

Pretreat fabric; make pattern alterations if combining dress and blouse styles.

Thursday:

Cut out dress, mark, and interface appropriate pieces; make Sashiko sampler to work out stitch arrangement and needle/bobbin tension.

Friday:

Create Sashiko design and transfer to dress front.

Saturday:

Stitch design; tie off ends; interface knots on inside.

Sunday:

Assemble dress; hem.

Homage to Matisse
DESIGNER:
Joneen M. Sargent

This dress is a beautiful canvas for the designer's artistic image created in free-form machine embroidery. The small self-fabric "packages" add interest to the skirt, meandering around the side and disappearing from sight at the hem.

Designer comments

"Upon viewing some of Matisse's early pen and ink drawings, I was taken by an etching entitled 'Marguerite Reading.' This so reminded me of my own daughter, I felt moved to capture this essence in my own way. But after completing the dress, I felt something was still missing. I decided to add more mystery by attaching the fabric packages—everyone loves the suspense of unopened boxes secured with string!"

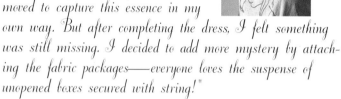

Materials and supplies

- Tent dress or jumper pattern
- Fabric of choice
- Water soluble stabilizer
- Silk finish thread for machine embroidery
- Machine embroidery hoop
- Topstitching needle
- Darning foot
- Fray retardant

Pattern and design changes

1. Although the pattern the designer used calls for pockets to be cut from the same fabric as the dress, she substituted lining material. The pockets then do not "catch" on the inside of the skirt, disrupting the way the dress hangs.

Construction details

1. Do not cut out the front bodice piece. Instead, trace it onto a piece of fabric large enough to accommodate the embroidery design and fit into the embroidery hoop. The larger piece provides a bit of extra bulk required by fabric manipulation and also allows for some pulling up caused by the decorative stitching.

2. Trace your artwork onto the stabilizer.

3. Secure fabric and stabilizer in embroidery hoop; two layers of stabilizer may be needed if the fabric is very delicate.

4. To prepare sewing machine for free-motion embroidery, lower the feed dogs, slightly reduce top tension, and use topstitching needle, darning foot, and silk-finish thread.

5. Pull bobbin thread up through fabric and stabilizer. Secure thread ends with fingertip and begin "painting," following the outlines of your design. Keep lines of stitching close together and as even as possible.

6. When through stitching, carefully apply fray retardant to wrong side of decorative stitching; let dry thoroughly.

7. Carefully remove embroidery hoop and trim away excess stabilizer.

8. Cut out bodice front piece and assemble dress.

9. When dress is complete, soak and rinse thoroughly to remove remaining stabilizer. Blot in towel, shape, and let dry.

For self-fabric packages:

1. Cut fabric squares ranging in sizes from 1¼" (3 cm) to 2" (5 cm).

2. Ravel edges to approximately ¼" (6 mm) of fringe.

3. Fold the four corners into the center. See Figure 1. Pin securely.

4. Use decorative thread to sew squares to dress in an arrangement of your choice, stitching through the centers of the folded edges to make a cross in the center of each square.

Tips from the designer

■ Many patterns call for bias tape to finish neck and armhole edges. If commercial brands seem too stiff for the dress fabric, make custom bias strips from a fabric of your choice (I used my husband's discarded neckties).

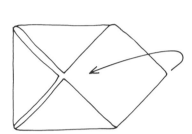

Fig. 1.
To make the self-fabric packages, cut fabric squares of varying sizes and fold the four corners into the center. Then, sew the folded squares to the dress in an arrangement of your choice.

Plan for the week

Monday:

Tuesday:

Wednesday:

Thursday:
Pretreat fabric; experiment with free-form machine embroidery to work out stitch settings.

Friday:
Cut fabric rectangle for front bodice; trace and stitch embroidery design.

Saturday:
Cut out dress, mark, and interface appropriate pieces; begin dress assembly.

Sunday:
Complete assembly; hem; make and attach self-fabric packages.

Petals 'n Lace

DESIGNER:
Karen M. Bennett

This lovely dress with tatted collar edging proves that it's easy to add something special to a standard pattern and make it your own original design. You could also edge the collar with lace, ribbon trim, or a creative arrangement of buttons.

Designer comments

"I love scalloped edges, so I created a scalloped collar for this dress and accentuated the curves with tatting. If you see something you like, try it—you will be surprised and delighted with the results."

Materials and supplies

- Pattern for tent or dress with buttoned front opening
- Fabric of choice
- Four pearl buttons

For tatting:

- Size 12 pearl cotton
- Glass beads

Tools

- Tatting shuttle
- Beading needle

Pattern and design changes

1. The designer added waist darts to the front and back bodice for a more fitted look, as for the Mammy's Garden dress on page 72.

2. She lengthened the sleeves by several inches and included a 1¼" (3 cm) hem so the linen fabric would hang better.

3. She changed the pattern's scoop neck to a V-neck and created a collar with a scalloped or petal-shaped edge.

4. She closed the front opening of the skirt.

Construction details

1. To change the scoop neck to a V-neck, redraw the neckline from shoulder seams to center front.

2. To create the new scalloped collar, overlap the front and back bodice, matching the shoulder seamlines; trace the new collar shape on fresh pattern paper placed over the overlapped front and back bodice pieces. See Figure 1.

3. To create the collar scallops or petal shapes, use a saucer or other round object to draw the curved collar edge. See Figure 2.

Tatted collar edging

■ Thread beads onto pearl cotton with beading needle. You will need about 30" (76 cm) of beads. Wind shuttle with thread and 15" (38 cm) of beads. DO NOT cut thread. There should be 15" (38 cm) of beads on the shuttle and 15" (38 cm) of beads on the thread.

```
*R      3 − 3 • 3 −3 cl
R       3 + 3 − 3 • 1 • 1•3 − 3 − 3 cl
R       3 + 3 • 3 − 3 cl
RW      ch 6 • 1 • 1 • 6
RW      R 6 + 6 cl
R       6 − 6 cl
RW      ch 6 •1 • 1 • 6*
```

Repeat * to * for desired length. Tatted edging shown is approximately 50" (127 cm).

■ For more information about tatting:

Jones, Rebecca. *The Complete Book of Tatting.*
London:Dryad Press Ltd., 1985.

Tips from the designer

■ Baste and try on as you go, especially if you've made changes to the pattern. It's worth the little bit of extra time to ensure the best fit.

■ Press, press, press! Pressing is the difference between "homemade" and "handmade."

Plan for the week

Monday

Tuesday:
Pretreat fabric.

Wednesday:
Make pattern changes and draw collar.

Thursday:
Cut out dress, mark, and interface appropriate pieces; begin tatting.

Friday:
Continue tatting.

Saturday:
Complete tatting; begin dress assembly.

Sunday:
Complete assembly; attach tatting to collar; cover buttons; hem.

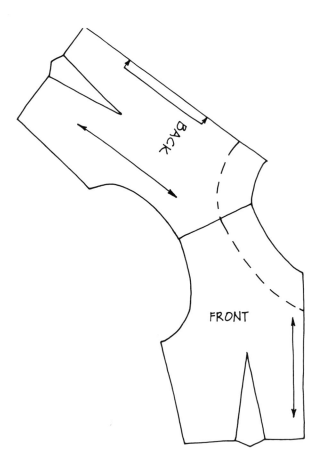

Fig. 1.
Match front and back shoulder seamlines, and trace the desired collar shape onto pattern paper.

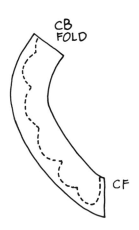

Fig. 2.
Use a saucer or other round object to draw the curved collar scallops.

Patchwork Plus
DESIGNER:
Sherida Ann Stone

If you fall in love with lots of different fabrics, here's a great way to use them all—piece together various combinations for interest. Then use a complementary solid for the contrasting bands to tie them all together.

Designer comments

"I love Seminole patchwork. It inspires me to invent interesting combinations of different fabrics."

Materials

- Tent or "big" dress pattern
- Fabric of choice
- Two buttons for waistline accent

Pattern and design changes

1. The designer shortened this very long dress by 3" (7.5 cm), for walking comfort.

2. She sectioned the skirt pattern to make room for the pieced squares and contrasting bands.

3. She cut the neckline facing and sleeve bands out of a solid complementary fabric, and applied them to the right side so they would show.

Construction details

1. For contrast band at neckline, pin right side of facing to wrong side of bodice neck edge. See Figure 1. When stitched and turned, it will appear on the outside of the garment, as a reverse facing.

2. Before sewing the pieced section of the skirt, study your arrangement of fabrics. The various patterns will look different when viewed together and after adding the solid bands in between.

Tips from the designer

■ If you are making a lot of changes to the pattern, whether to alter the fit or change the design, use a non-fusible interfacing and trace the pattern pieces first. Then make the changes on the interfacing version, saving the original pattern for later use. Also, if you make any mistakes, you still have the original pattern intact.

■ When I'm thinking about pieced designs, I staple fabric scraps to small index cards and carry them with me when I'm searching for new combinations at the fabric stores. I also visit my fabric-aholic friends to look through their scrap baskets.

▨ RIGHT SIDE
☐ WRONG SIDE, BODICE
▨ WRONG SIDE, FACING

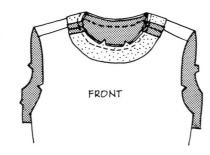

FRONT

Fig. 1.
To create a reverse facing, stitch the right side of the facing to the wrong side of the garment. When turned to the outside, the right side of the facing will show.

Plan for the week

Monday:

Tuesday:

Wednesday:

Thursday:

Friday:
Pretreat fabric; make pattern alterations; experiment with pieced fabric arrangements.

Saturday:
Cut out dress, mark, and interface appropriate pieces; cut out fabric squares and bands for pieced section; piece skirt.

Sunday:
Assemble dress; hem; attach button trim.

Summer Showers

DESIGNER:
Joneen M. Sargent

The pockets on this dress are bright spots of color as well as showcases for your pieced designs. An added bonus is that the easy technique you use to make them improves your quilting skills!

Designer comments

"On a cold, snowy day in January, I felt the urge to think about warm weather and bright spring colors. I chose this pattern because of the simple cut of the dress and the large pockets to display the pieced umbrellas. After the dress was assembled, I rushed off to my favorite fabric store to find the perfect buttons—and there they were waiting for me."

Materials and supplies

- Tent dress or jumper pattern
- Fabric of choice
- Coordinating fabrics for piecework pockets
- Paper piecing patterns of choice, available from quilting shops, with enough copies to complete the project
- Lining fabric for pockets (optional)

Tools

- Small bright light near sewing machine
- Moist sponge
- Tweezers

Pattern and design changes

The basic pattern was modified to provide a lining for the pockets, because the rough edges of the fabric piecing would be visible on the inside of the pockets if not lined. An alternative would be to use muslin instead of paper as the piecing design base; muslin would not be removed, as the paper is, and would be smooth inside the pockets.

Construction details

1. Choose and assemble paper piecing blocks according to package instructions. A small bright light is helpful to see through the paper to the sewing lines. Carefully press each new addition of fabric without steam, to avoid stretching the fabric.

2. Add border edges to pieced blocks, if necessary, to approximate pocket sizes plus seam allowances.

3. When all piecing blocks are completed, remove the paper backing by wiping the paper with a moist sponge and tearing away the pieces in reverse order of assembly (last piece first). Use tweezers to remove any paper fragments left behind.

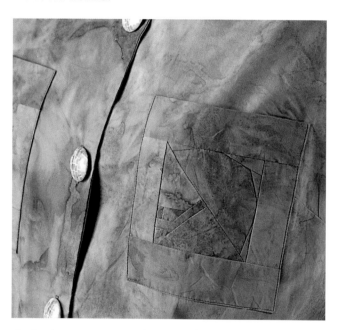

4. Cut lining pieces to the size of the completed pockets plus seam allowances. Sew top edges of lining and pocket facing, right sides together. Press seam and pocket facing foldline.

5. Right sides together, stitch lining to pocket from top foldline to bottom of pocket along side seamlines; leave a small opening at bottom of pocket.

6. Turn pocket to right side through small opening, hand-stitch opening closed, and press carefully.

7. Pin pockets to dress fronts; topstitch side and bottom edges.

8. Finish assembling garment.

Tips from the designer

■ Give the new paper piecing patterns a try. They are available in many designs and "pictures," and they enable the quilting novice to achieve sharp points and accurate reproduction of the design with minimal practice.

Plan for the week

Monday:

∼∼∽∾

Tuesday:
Pretreat fabric.

Wednesday:
Cut out dress, mark, and interface appropriate pieces.

Thursday:
Begin making paper piecing blocks for pockets.

Friday:
Complete paper piecing blocks.

Saturday:
Assemble pockets and sew to dress fronts.

Sunday:
Complete dress assembly; make buttonholes and sew on buttons; hem.

Material Magic

DESIGNER:

Mary S. Parker

In this colorful jumper, pleating is used both for its decorative effect and for gathering in the fullness of the pattern. This is a great example of putting function to work in a beautiful way.

Designer comments

"I've seen fabric manipulation techniques to create interesting textures on garments such as vests. I thought about capturing the decorative aspect of pleating while also using it to perform its basic purpose—and it works well!"

Materials and supplies

■ Tent dress or jumper pattern, preferably one that uses pleats at the bodice/skirt seam instead of gathers

■ Fabric of choice, preferably one that is lightweight enough to drape well

■ Heavy-duty spray starch

■ Rayon embroidery thread

■ Bobbin fill thread for use when rayon embroidery thread is in the needle

■ Regular weight thread to match fabric

Tools

■ Optional pleater board, available from sewing supply stores or mail order suppliers

Pattern and design changes

1. Pleating was used both decoratively and to gather in the fullness of the skirt. Therefore, the seam joining the bodice to the skirt was omitted.

2. The designer also replaced the pattern's patch pockets with in-seam side pockets, so the pockets would not detract from the manipulated fabric effect.

Construction details

1. If the dress or jumper pattern you select has pleats marked in the skirt where it joins the bodice, pin these together along the stitching lines. Then pin the bodice front to the skirt front, and the bodice back to the skirt back. Measure the distance from the highest point on the pattern (usually the neck edge of the shoulder seam) down to the bodice/skirt dividing line. Measure both the pattern back and front, because these may be different. Set pinned pattern aside.

2. Cut the neck and armhole facings out of the fashion fabric. Do not cut out the front facings yet; you can cut them from the excess selvage fabric left after pleating and cutting the jumper fronts and backs.

3. Divide the remaining fabric into four pieces of equal length. For an ankle-length jumper, the pieces should be about 1⅜ yards (1.3 m) long.

4. Experiment with folding lengthwise pleats of varying widths in the upper portion of one piece of the fashion fabric. If your fabric has a definite stripe, this can serve as your pleating guide. Otherwise, you can use a pleating guide to achieve consistent spacing and depth without a lot of measuring. Once you have decided on pleat depth and spacing, pin the pleats in the upper part of the fabric, down to the measurement you took in step #1. See Figure 1.

5. Lay the pinned front pattern piece on top of the pleated fabric, with the bodice portion over the pleated area. Make a chalk outline around the outside edge, then fold down the bodice part of the pattern and use a horizontal line of pins to indicate where the bodice would normally meet the skirt. Set pattern piece aside.

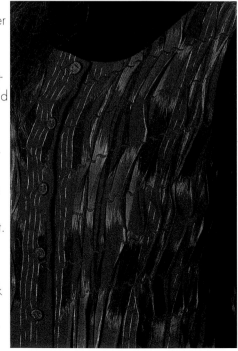

6. Extend the chalk outline down the length of fabric for the front opening and side edges. Measure between these two lines at the bottom of the fabric to determine what the skirt width will be, and then measure the width of the skirt pattern piece. If these two measurements are very close, the pleating will result in a jumper that has the same amount of design ease as the pattern. If they differ considerably, think about a different pleating scheme. If more fabric is present in the skirt area than the pattern calls for, you'll need to release some of the pleating; to do this, allow more space between the pleats or make them shallower. If not enough fabric is present, increase the number of pleats or make them deeper.

7. When you've determined a pleating scheme that will work with your jumper pattern, remove any pins, form the pleats, spray them with heavy duty starch, and iron to set them. Depending on the fabric, you may wish to repeat this several times.

8. Pin the bodice pattern piece to the pleated fabric panel to verify that the chalk lines you drew earlier are still accurate; you may need to re-chalk the outline if it is no longer visible. Re-pin the dividing line between bodice and skirt—this is where you will end the stitching as you sew the pleats down. You may also want to insert pins at intervals in the pleats to hold them in place as you sew (remember to remove pins before you sew over them).

9. Decide on the angle of stitching across the pleats; note that the degree of tilt from the horizontal axis will determine the final pleat depth. On the jumper shown, the pleats on the front (left) are shallower because they are sewn in lines that are closer to horizontal than the much deeper pleats on the back (right). Draw the preferred stitching angle on the pattern and then draw parallel lines 2" (5 cm) away from it all over the bodice area, each

one ending at the bodice/skirt dividing line.

10. Fold back the pattern along each marked line one by one and lightly chalk the fabric along the folded-back pattern.

11. Select an appropriate decorative stitch. With rayon embroidery thread in the needle and an appropriate bobbin thread, stitch along every other marked chalk line; your stitching lines will be 4" (10 cm) apart. Be sure to end your stitching at the horizontal row of pins that marks the end of the bodice area and the beginning of the skirt (give yourself a little leeway, however, in case the fabric has changed dimensions during the pleating).

12. After stitching every other line, press the pleats in the opposite direction between the rows of stitching. Note that you will lose the marked chalk lines you made previously, so you will either need to re-mark the intervening stitching lines or use a sewing machine attachment to guide you while sewing them.

13. Stitch the in-between lines with the same rayon embroidery thread. You now have stitched lines 2" (5 cm) apart.

14. Pin the front pattern piece to the pleated and stitched fabric and cut the bodice portion out, continuing to cut down the straight of grain on both front opening and side seam. Cut the front facings out of the excess fabric along the selvages.

15. Repeat steps #5 through #14 for the other three fabric panels (one more for the front and two for the back). By chalking the sewing lines on each piece separately, using the pattern pieces as a guide, you should end up with symmetrical lines on both sides of the garment.

16. Assemble the dress.

Tips from the designer

■ Make several samples of pleated fabric to test how various embroidery stitches behave and to get comfortable with the manipulation technique.

■ Use a stiffer interfacing for the neck and armhole facings, to support the heavier weight of the pleated fabric.

Plan for the week

Monday:

Tuesday:

Wednesday:

Thursday:
Pretreat fabric; measure pattern to determine pleated area.

Friday:
Experiment with pleating arrangements; cut out neck and armhole facings.

Saturday:
Pleat and mark fabric panels; stitch pleats for front and back bodices; cut out front and back pieces.

Sunday:
Cut and interface front facings; assemble dress; make buttonholes and sew on buttons; hem.

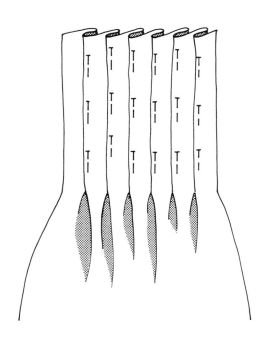

Fig. 1.
After deciding on a pleating depth and spacing, pin the pleats in the upper part of the fabric panel. This is where the bodice piece will be positioned.

Polka Dot Pizzazz

DESIGNER:
M. Luanne Carson

This simple dress is made from a delectably swirly rayon. for a beautiful and fluid look. The pleated collar and tucked sleeve hems make for a perfect complement to the released tucks of the skirt.

Designer comments

"In a recent class I taught that emphasized embellishment, one of my students chose to work with the Perfect Pleater™. When I started this dress, it occurred to me that pleating the collar would be a great creative option."

Materials

■ Pattern for princess seam released-tuck dress

■ Fabric of choice, including extra yardage for pleating

Tools

■ Fabric pleater

Pattern and design changes

1. The designer cut the upper collar from pleated self-fabric and extended the sleeve length to accommodate the pleated hem.

2. She also straightened the underarm sleeve seams, to accommodate the greater bulk of the tucked hem and complement the fluid look of the entire dress.

Construction details

1. Use the pleater to create enough pleated fabric for the selected pattern piece, plus a 1" (2.5 cm) margin around all edges.

2. If the pattern piece you will be pleating exceeds the dimensions of the pleater, you may have to pleat the fabric in sections. For example, the collar of this dress was longer than the 11" (28 cm) pleater. Therefore, the designer pleated one end of the flat fabric, pressed the pleats well, and then gently removed the fabric from the pleater. She fused a piece of knit interfacing to the back side of the pleats, leaving 1" (2.5 cm) adjacent to the unpleated portion free—so she could gently tuck the unpleated section back into the pleater to complete the process. She then pressed and interfaced the remaining end of the fabric.

3. Place the upper collar pattern on the pleated fabric and cut out. The under collar need not be pleated.

4. Proceed with standard collar assembly and application.

To tuck and hem sleeve:

1. Turn under hem allowance and press; turn under again and press. The raw edge is now butted into the second fold Stitch tuck the desired distance from folded edge and turn remaining hem back down. See Figure 1.

Tips from the designer

■ Experiment with the pleater, tucking the fabric under different arrangements of the pleater's louvers, until you get an effect you like.

■ Be careful estimating how much extra length you will need to add to the sleeve. Remember that a ¼" (6 mm) tuck uses up ½" (1.25 cm) of fabric.

Plan for the week

Monday:

Tuesday:

Wednesday:

Thursday:
Pretreat fabric.

Friday:
Cut out dress, mark, and interface appropriate pieces; experiment with pleating arrangements.

Saturday:
Pleat fabric and assemble collar; begin dress assembly.

Sunday:
Complete assembly; make buttonholes; sew on buttons; hem.

Fig. 1.
To create tucked hem in a standard sleeve (A), fold under along hemline and press (B). Fold under again, press, and stitch tuck (C). Turn remaining hem back down (D).

A
HEMLINE

B

C

D

Tapestry of Gold
DESIGNER:
Linda Boyd

Use invisible thread to stitch decorative cords onto the collar and create a lovely painterly effect for this feminine princess seam dress. Then. plan a pretty surprise for the back.

Designer comments

"I liked the effect of making fabric-wrapped cording for the back ties to echo the decorative cords on the collar."

Materials and supplies

- Pattern for princess style dress with back ties
- Fabric of choice, contrast fabric for collar
- Three different lightweight decorative cords for collar embellishment
- Invisible thread for stitching decorative cords
- Gold-colored buttons to accent metallic gold cord
- ¼" (6 mm) cording
- Tear-away stabilizer

Tools

- Turning tool for fabric tubes
- Bodkin for threading cording in fabric tubes

Pattern and design changes

1. The designer cut the upper collar/collar facing pieces from contrast fabric, as a background for the decorative cords, and added piping to the collar edge.

2. She replaced the pattern's back ties with fabric loops and lacing.

3. She eliminated the pattern's pockets, for a sleek side seam.

Construction Details

1. Mark placement of loops along back princess seamlines at waistline, 1" (2.5 cm) below waistline, and five points above waistline at 1" (2.5 cm) intervals.

2. Make and turn bias fabric tubes and thread with ¼" (6 mm) cording. Use fourteen 2½" (6.5 cm) corded tubes for loops, fold in half, and baste them where marked at back seam. Use one 3½-yard (3.2-m) corded tube for lacing. Finish ends by stitching across both fabric and cording at one end; gently pull opposite end of cord out of fabric tube about 2" (5 cm) and stitch across cording and fabric; gently ease fabric tube over raw end until it disappears inside.

For collar:

1. Drape decorative cords as desired on right side of contrast collar pieces. Remember that the cord you drape first will be on the bottom; the cord you drape last will be on the top and the most visible.

2. Cover collar pieces with a sheet of tear-away stabilizer and pin in place.

3. Thread machine with invisible thread on top and bobbin thread to match fabric; loosen top tension slightly.

4. Lightly mark first few rows, ¼" (6 mm) apart, along lengthwise grain; using a straight stitch, sew collar pieces in parallel rows.

5. Carefully tear away stabilizer, lightly press underside of collar pieces with pressing cloth and warm iron.

6. Stitch collar pieces in opposite direction, along crosswise grain, ¼" (6 mm) apart.

7. Use a 43" (109 cm) corded strip to pipe collar edge before attaching collar/facing to dress.

Tips from the designer

■ When stitching the narrow strips for the fabric tubes, use a narrow short zigzag. This keeps the thread from popping while turning the tube.

■ Try the dress on before putting the sleeves in, to check the fit; this saves you from having to redo sleeve insertion, everybody's least favorite step.

Plan for the week

Monday:

Tuesday:

Wednesday:
Pretreat fabric; make pattern changes; experiment with thread embroidery.

Thursday:
Cut out dress, mark, and interface appropriate pieces.

Friday:
Embroider and assemble collar.

Saturday:
Begin dress assembly; make bias loops and back lacing.

Sunday:
Complete assembly, inserting bias loops in back seams; lace tie ends through loops; make buttonholes and sew on buttons; hem.

Summertime Glow
DESIGNER:
M. Luanne Carson

This summery dress uses strips of leftover fabric to create a simple and pretty neckline ruffle, topped off with a fabric flower.

Designer comments

"This pattern was designed with off-the-shoulder flutters of fabric, which meant I would have to wear a strapless bra. I knew right then that the dress would probably stay in the closet, so I made some basic changes to be able to wear it with regular undergarments."

Materials and supplies

- Pattern for princess seam off-the-shoulder dress
- Fabric of choice
- ¼" (6 mm) or ⅜" (1 cm) elastic

Tools

- Blind stitch sewing machine foot or attachment
- Decorative sewing machine foot of choice
- Gathering attachment or sewing machine foot (optional)

Pattern and design changes

The designer replaced the off-the-shoulder pattern's fabric "flutters" with fabric straps wide enough to cover bra straps.

Construction details

1. Piece strips of fabric together end-to-end, to create a large circle

2. Blind-stitch both raw edges of the fabric circle, for a scalloped effect.

3. Randomly tuck the circle to a size that will cross the front neckline, create both straps, and drape down below the back neckline in a free-hanging necklace.

4. Stitch the tucks in place down the center of the circular strip, using a decorative stitch and thread color picked up from the fabric's design. The result will look like a ruffle.

5. Try the assembled dress on and arrange the ruffle to fit comfortably over the shoulders; hand-tack the ruffle to the upper corners of the back and the front scoop neckline.

6. Catch-stitch elastic to underside of straps, from front to back shoulder; this allows for comfort of motion and helps fabric straps retain their original dimension.

For the flower:

1. Out of fabric scraps, cut strips 2" (5 cm) wide by about 20" (51 cm) long.

2. Round the corners of one long edge and blind-stitch raw edge, for a scalloped effect.

3. Gather other long edge tightly, drawing up strip into a curl.

4. Roll gathered strip into flower shape and hand-tack to dress neckline. Note that the tightly gathered edge, when rolled up, looks like the pistil at the center of a flower.

Tips from the designer

■ When trying on the dress to determine how long the ruffled straps need to be so that they fit comfortably over the shoulders, don't forget to experiment with range of motion—raise your arms, reach out and up, roll your shoulders.

■ When hemming a knit fabric, use two rows of double-needle stitching to provide enough weight to keep the hem from rolling up.

Plan for the week

Monday:

∾∾∾∾

Tuesday:

∾∾∾∾

Wednesday:

∾∾∾∾

Thursday:
Pretreat fabric.

Friday:
Cut out dress, mark, and interface appropriate pieces.

Saturday:
Make fabric ruffle; begin dress assembly.

Sunday:
Complete assembly; attach ruffle and elastic; make and attach fabric flower; hem.

Summer in the City
DESIGNER:
Mary S. Parker

For quick dressing as well as quick construction, here's a dress that incorporates its own coordinating vest front. Without double layers of fabric at the back, it's cooler to wear on a hot day.

Designer comments

"As you can probably tell, I had a lot of fun piecing coordinating fabrics for the vest on this dress. The creative possibilities are endless!"

Materials and supplies

- Pattern for princess seam dress
- Vest pattern
- Fabric of choice for dress
- Coordinating fabrics for pieced vest fronts

Pattern and design changes

The designer used the vest front pieces from a separate pattern and attached them at the shoulders and side seams of the dress pattern.

Construction details

1. Make sure the dress and vest patterns are compatible in armhole depth and width at the shoulder. To do this, pin vest front pattern pieces to the dress front bodice pattern, matching shoulder seamlines and center fronts. The front bodice pattern should extend at least ½" (1.25 cm) on each side of the vest front at the shoulder seam. If it does not, try another vest pattern or narrow the shoulder of the vest. The vest armhole should be at least ½" (1.25 cm) larger than the dress armhole. See Figure 1.

2. Complete vest front according to pattern instructions, omitting references to vest back. For vest front lining, use dress fabric. Make buttonholes and sew on buttons.

3. Complete as much of the dress as you can without

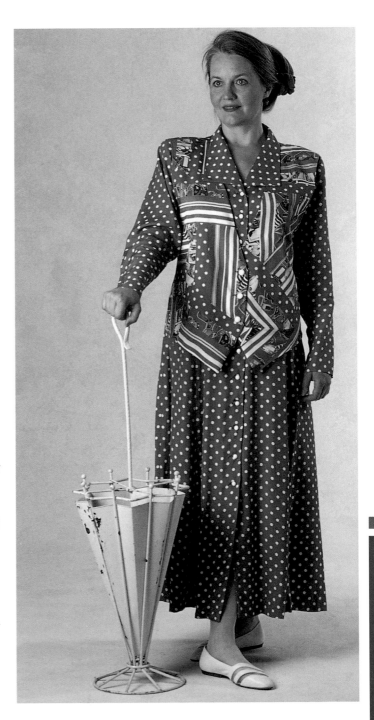

sewing the side seams. For example, sew the princess seams, attach collar and facings, make buttonholes, and sew on buttons. Set in the majority of the sleeve, except the area at the very bottom of the armhole.

4. Baste completed vest fronts to dress front at shoulders.

5. Pin-baste the dress side seams, leaving vest sides free, and try it on. Button both the dress and the vest. Arrange the vest sides into the most flattering position and pin in place. NOTE: A sewing friend is very helpful here, but if you are alone, pin the vest to the dress along the sides, leaving various amounts of ease, until you find the most flattering line.

6. Pin the vest sides to the dress slightly in front of the pin-basted side seams, so you can remove the side seam pins without removing the vest pins.

7. Take off the dress and remove side seam pins. Baste the vest to the dress within the seam allowance, according to the placement you determined when you tried on the dress.

8. Complete the dress, sewing up the side seams, sleeve seams, and remaining armhole seam.

Tips from the designer

■ The attached vest can be made from a single coordinating fabric or pieced from many fabrics, as shown here. If you create custom-pieced fabric, stabilize it by fusing lightweight interfacing to the wrong sides of the vest fronts before lining them.

■ If the front opening of your pattern is on the straight of grain, it does not include walking ease to keep the dress from separating when you move. This is my method of adding walking ease: place a yardstick along the front edge, with the top at the neckline or the first straight section of the front edge if the neckline has a fold-back collar. Rotate out the bottom end of the yardstick, holding the top end in place, until it is approximately 1 1/2" (4 cm) away from the pattern at the knee. Draw a new front edge, continuing the line down to the bottom of the garment.

Plan for the week

Monday:

Tuesday:

Wednesday:
Pretreat fabrics; make alterations to vest pattern, if necessary.

Thursday:
Piece coordinating fabrics for vest fronts.

Friday:
Cut out vest fronts and dress, mark, and interface appropriate pieces; assemble lined vest fronts; make buttonholes and sew on buttons.

Saturday:
Begin dress assembly; make buttonholes and sew on buttons; attach and adjust vest fronts.

Sunday:
Complete assembly; hem.

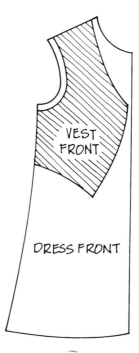

Fig. 1.
When combining a vest pattern with a dress pattern, be sure that the vest front is narrower at the shoulder seam and larger around the armhole.

Pretty in Pink

DESIGNER:
Elizabeth Searle

This pink silk dress is as fresh and pretty as a spring morning with petal sleeves that are both interesting and flattering.

Designer comments

"I call this my 'uniform' dress because I've made it so many different ways (24 times in the last 5 years!), and it's so comfortable to wear. This version is made out of pink silk, but I've also made it in gingham (see page 107), chambray, linen with buttons down the front, cotton prints, rayon, and lightweight denim; with long sleeves, short sleeves, and the tulip or petal sleeves shown here; for myself, a client, my sisters, and my mother. A truly versatile style that's easy to fit to different figure types and a pleasure to wear!"

Materials and supplies

■ Pattern for princess seam dress

■ Fabric of choice, including a little extra for redesigned sleeves

■ Lining fabric for redesigned sleeves

Pattern and design changes

1. The designer started with a basic princess dress pattern, and then redrew the sleeve pattern pieces to form a one-part wrapped petal sleeve. See Figure 1.

2. She also lined the sleeve for a clean finish and to reduce the bulk of a hem.

Construction details

1. Assemble dress up to sleeve insertion, according to pattern instructions.

2. Right sides together, stitch lining to sleeve around outside edge.

3. Trim, turn, and press. Baste raw edges together.

4. Ease sleeve into armhole, lapping front "petal" over back, or back over front depending on your preference. Match shoulder points and notches, and baste in place before stitching.

Tips from the designer

■ This simple, classic dress style offers lots of opportunities for creative alteration and embellishment. For example, when I made it out of lightweight denim, I thought the front looked too plain, so I added lace appliqué around the neckline for an interesting effect. Strike out on your own and explore unusual combinations.

Plan for the week

Monday:

Tuesday:

Wednesday:

Thursday:

Friday:

Pretreat fabric; draw petal sleeve pattern.

Saturday:

Cut out sleeve and remaining dress pieces, mark, and interface appropriate pieces; assemble and line sleeve; begin dress assembly.

Sunday:

Complete assembly; hem.

SHOULDER POINT

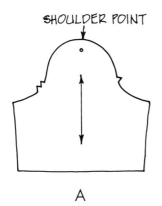 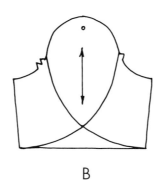 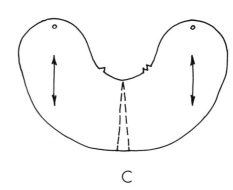

A   B   C

Fig. 1.

To transform a standard sleeve into a petal sleeve, first mark the shoulder point on the original pattern piece, if not already indicated (A). Trace two mirror-image "petals" from armhole edges just above the notches to lower edge (B). Cut out two petal patterns and match them at the underarm, keeping grainlines parallel. Place on fabric and cut as one piece, filling in at hem (C).

Dance All Night

DESIGNER:
Tracy Munn

When you want to whip up a new dress to go dancing in, use a familiar pattern that will go together fast—and make a few changes to get the results you want. Spend your time twirling around the dance floor, not in the sewing room.

Designer comments

"I've already made this pattern, so I know it will look and fit great. Why reinvent the wheel by starting with a new pattern? I just make a few changes to give me the features I want. In this case, I wanted to show off some gorgeous silver buttons, and I wanted the dress to swish and swirl on the dance floor."

Materials and supplies

- Pattern for princess seam dress
- Fabric of choice
- Unique buttons of choice

Pattern and design changes

1. The designer started with a basic princess dress pattern with the front cut on the fold and a zipper closure in the back. She changed the zippered back opening to a buttoned front opening, to showcase some special buttons.

2. She also cut the neckline lower and wider, for evening, and replaced the neck facing and sleeve hem with bias bands that complement the front button band.

Construction details

1. Instead of placing the dress front piece on the fold, cut the piece out twice (for a right and left

front). Add 2" (5 cm) to the center front of each piece, for the button placket. The designer chose a fabric that allowed her to turn the fabric to the outside and edgestitch close to both sides for a mock placket.

2. To make the neckline band, cut a piece of bias self-fabric the length of the neckline and 2" (5 cm) wide, like the front button placket. Stitch to the neckline's wrong side, turn to the right side, and edgestitch close to both edges.

3. Make the sleeve bands like the neckline band, cut to the same circumference as the sleeve and 2" (5 cm) wide.

Tips from the designer

■ Bias bands are a great way to finish seams—they are neat, clean, and easy. And they never flop out to the right side like facings. An added bonus is that they also create a decorative effect, so think about using contrasting fabrics for your bias edgings or contrasting thread for the edgestitching.

Plan for the week

Monday:

Tuesday:

Wednesday:

Thursday:

Friday:
Pretreat fabric; make pattern alterations.

Saturday:
Cut out dress, mark, and interface appropriate pieces; begin dress assembly.

Sunday:
Complete assembly; make buttonholes and sew on buttons; hem.

Chiffon à la Mode
DESIGNER:
Elizabeth Searle

Designer comments

"I like experimenting with contrasts, such as patterns with solids, structured with drapey, feminine with tailored. There are just so many options for interesting results."

Materials and supplies

■ Pattern for princess seam dress

■ Fabric of choice

■ Approximately ½ yard (.5 m) chiffon

Pattern and design changes

The designer started with a basic princess dress pattern, which she altered by adding a series of buttonholes around the neckline for the chiffon "necklace" accent.

Construction details

1. Cut three pieces of chiffon approximately 6" (15 cm) wide by 45" (115 cm) long. Stitch together and turn inside out to make tubes. The two tubes for use as tie ends in the back should be stitched at an angle at one end; the straight ends are sewn into the side waist seams.

2. Make an even number of buttonholes, approximately ⅝" (1.5 cm) long, through both the dress and neckline facing. Make sure the buttonholes are evenly distributed around the neckline.

3. Thread the third chiffon tube through the buttonholes and whipstitch the ends together inside, at the back. The small buttonhole size will constrict the chiffon tube and cause it to puff out.

The creative combination of checked gingham and solid chiffon in this dress is both unusual and interesting. The chiffon dresses up the gingham, while the gingham creates a casual background for the chiffon.

Tips from the designer

■ Another option is to make the third chiffon tube longer and thread through the buttonholes so the ends hang free in the front and can be tied in a pretty bow.

Plan for the week

Monday:

Tuesday:

Wednesday:

Thursday:

Friday:
Pretreat fabric.

Saturday:
Make chiffon tubes; cut out dress, mark, and interface appropriate pieces.

Sunday:
Assemble dress; make buttonholes; thread chiffon tube through buttonholes; hem.

Seersucker Rainbow

DESIGNER:
M. Luanne Carson

This unusual shirtwaist style with hidden front opening and side tucks creates a bib-like bodice that is perfect for showing off the appliquéd self-fabric tubes. The removable brooch creates an artistic focal point and covers the ending point of the fabric tubes.

Designer comments

"After completing this dress, I was disappointed in its effect—there was nothing special about it. It seemed too staid and traditional, so I invented ways to make it more whimsical and fun even though I had only scraps of fabric left to work with."

Materials and supplies

- Pattern for shirtwaist dress with bib front
- Fabric of choice, including extra for belt and appliqué tubes
- Lightweight fabric for bodice facing
- Optional contrasting fabric for appliqué tubes
- Assorted buttons and leather scraps for brooch
- Belting material and buckle
- Hook-and-loop dots for fabric tube and belt closures

Construction details

1. Make bias tubes of varying widths and lengths out of scraps of fabric. See Figure 1. Note that the puckered nature of the seersucker fabric emphasizes the unevenness of the fabric tubes on this dress.

2. Arrange tubes in pleasing design on bodice and around neckline, overlapping ends to get continuous lines. Loosely knot tubes or lay them down in a loop-de-loop fashion for added interest and texture. Hand-tack tubes in place.

3. Create a removable brooch from miscellaneous buttons glued to scraps of leather. Instead of attaching a standard pin clasp to the back, which can damage the fabric after repeated use, use a large nylon snap to attach to the bodice front.

4. Cover belting with fabric; attach buckle at one end; keep tip of belt from sticking out with hook-and-loop dot.

Tips from the designer

- Make sure bodice front and back are lightly faced, to support the added weight and hand-tacking of the fabric tubes.

- For design interest, overlap the front opening of the bodice with the end of a fabric tube and attach to one side with a hook-and-loop dot; the overlap will be covered with the removable brooch.

- In a striped fabric, such as the seersucker used here, you can create subtle color effects by tucking up different stripes and stitching them to the inside. For example, in sections of this skirt, the light grey, violet, and gold stripes were tucked to the inside, to create broader bands of the navy and red than appear in the untucked fabric. This is an easy way to create custom yardage.

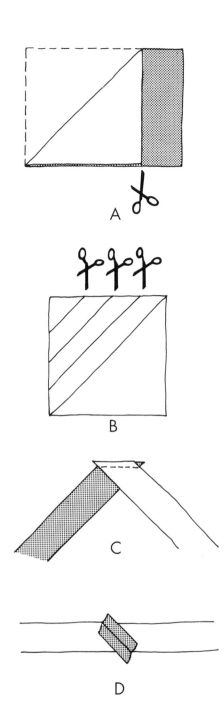

A

B

C

D

Plan for the week

Monday:

Tuesday:

Wednesday:
Pretreat fabric.

Thursday:
Tuck up stripes of fabric to create desired color effects; cut out dress, mark, and interface appropriate pieces.

Friday:
Begin dress assembly; make bias fabric tubes.

Saturday:
Complete assembly; drape and attach bias tubes to bodice front and back.

Sunday:
Make brooch; assemble belt; finish all closures; hem.

Fig. 1.
To make bias tubes, first determine bias of fabric by folding over corner to form an even triangle and cutting off excess (A). Cut bias strips of desired width out of resulting fabric square (B). Stitch ends of bias strips together (C)

Positive Piping
DESIGNER:
Joyce Baldwin

Piping is an attractive and easy way to add interest to the style lines of any pattern—just slash the pattern and add seam allowances to both slashed edges. It's also a decorative method of finishing seams.

Designer comments

"I still can't decide whether I should have piped the front opening edge. I guess I'll try that on the next dress."

Materials and supplies

■ Pattern for sleeveless shirtwaist with yoke bodice and elasticized waist

■ Fabric of choice

■ Contrast color piping or contrast fabric for custom-made piping

■ Nine contrast buttons

Tools

■ Piping insertion sewing machine foot, if available, or zipper foot

Pattern and design changes

The designer illustrates how older patterns, which are usually close-fitting, can be easily altered for the looser fit preferred today, and how piping can be used as a nice color accent. She changed the gathered and stitched waistline to an elasticized waistline, and slashed and spread the pattern in various places to add ease for greater wearing comfort. See Figure 1 for following construction details.

Construction details

1. Add ⅜" (1 cm) to seam allowances at all waistline edges, to provide sufficient width for elastic casing.

4. Increase size of armhole for more comfortable fit by adding ¼" (6 mm) at outer shoulder edge, tapering to zero at neck. Total armhole increase is ½" (1.25 cm).

4a. Slash and spread armhole facing ½" (1.25 cm) to correspond to shoulder alteration.

5. Add ⅜" (1 cm) to front and back bodice side seams and side seams of armhole facing, to increase size of armhole for comfort.

6. Lengthen front and back bodice and front facing 1" (2.5 cm) to increase blouson design fullness.

7. Slash and spread front and back bodice ¾" (2 cm) to increase design fullness.

8. Slash and spread front and back skirt so that skirt waistline equals bodice waistline. This results in increased design fullness and makes it easier to sew bodice and skirt together for elastic casing.

9. Slash along foldline of pocket facing and add seam allowance to both slashed edges, to create seam for piping insertion.

10. Overlap and tape pocket and pocket facing along stitching lines, to eliminate unnecessary seam.

11. If piping front opening edge, slash along foldline of skirt front facing and add seam allowances to both slashed edges.

Tips from the designer

■ Prewash purchased piping, or cord and fabric if you're making your own piping, to prevent puckering in the finished garment. If making your own, cut the fabric as much on the bias as possible, for maximum flexibility.

■ Don't forget to clip the fabric covering when piping around corners and curves.

■ To reduce piping bulk at the intersection of seams, clip the fabric covering and slide it back, so you can cut off the portion of the cord that extends into the seam allowance. See Figure 2.

2. Add ¼" (6 mm) to center back edges, to widen back shoulder yoke for more comfortable fit.

3. Slash and spread back yoke ¼" (6 mm) at lower edge, tapering to zero at shoulder edge, for more comfortable fit. Straighten lower edge of yoke; this will increase armhole by ⅛" (3 mm).

3a. Slash and spread armhole facing ⅛" (3 mm) to correspond to increase on yoke edge.

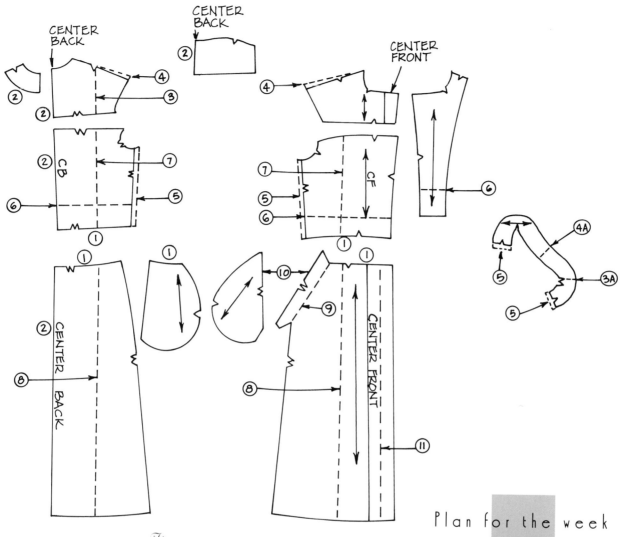

Fig. 1.
Alter a standard pattern to increase blouson fullness, add elastic casing at waistline, and accommodate piped seams. See "Construction details."

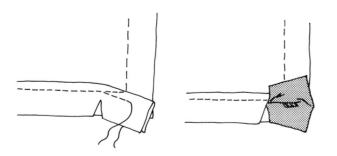

Fig. 2.
To reduce bulk where piped seams intersect (left), clip the fabric covering and slide it back, then trim off the end of the cording (right).

Plan for the week

Monday:

Tuesday:

Wednesday:
Pretreat fabric and cording.

Thursday:
Make pattern changes; assemble piping, if not using store-bought.

Friday:
Cut out dress, mark, and interface appropriate pieces.

Saturday:
Baste cording in place; begin dress assembly.

Sunday:
Finish assembly; make buttonholes and sew on buttons; hem.

Sweet Repeats

DESIGNER:
Linda Boyd

Easy and quick machine embroidery turns fabric as plain as denim into a very special dress, especially with a coordinated belt made out of leftover scraps. This is a great way to put your sewing machine's decorative stitches to work!

Designer comments

"I had to consider the time and cost available to spend on this dress, because I work full-time and sewing is my fun time. This embroidery design took less than three hours and was very inexpensive."

Materials and supplies

■ Pattern for shirtwaist dress with yoke back and elasticized waist

■ Fabric of choice

■ Variegated thread for machine embroidery

■ Spray or tear-away stabilizer for embroidered areas

■ 1½" (4 cm) belting

■ Hook-and-loop tape for belt closure

■ Coordinating buttons

Tools

■ Extra sharp needle, such as Jeans or Microtex, for embroidery

■ Satin stitch sewing machine foot or open embroidery foot, if available

■ Edgestitch foot, if available, to make topstitching easier and more accurate

Pattern and design changes

1. The designer first changed the grainlines on the skirt front and back pieces for a more flattering look. The grainline is redrawn down the center of the skirt pieces, instead of parallel to center front and center back. See Figure 1. She says the result is very slimming, especially if you have full hips. NOTE: Repositioning the pattern pieces this way may require more fabric, so check your pattern before buying material.

2. She then trimmed away ⅝" (1.5 cm) at the back waist, starting at center back and tapering to zero at the side seams. See Figure 2. She says that this alteration eliminates the little roll of fabric you often see below the belt, which results because many women are curved at the lower back waistline and the skirt is usually too long in this area.

Construction details

1. Do not cut out the bodice front pieces until completing the machine embroidery. You will do the embroidery on squares of fabric that are 2" (5 cm) larger than the pattern pieces all the way around.

2. Experiment with different decorative stitches and decide on placement of embroidery. The designer chose a daisy stitch and vine stitch.

3. Stabilize the squares of fabric for the bodice fronts and lightly mark embroidery placement.

4. Using variegated thread and satin stitch foot or embroidery foot, if available, carefully stitch all rows of embroidery on fabric squares.

5. Place bodice front pattern piece on one fabric square and arrange so that first embroidery row is 1¾" (4.5 cm) from center front; cut out bodice front. Reverse bodice front pattern piece on other fabric square for other side.

6. Assemble dress.

For the belt:

1. Cut one strip of leftover embroidered fabric, 12" (30.5 cm) by 4" (10 cm) for center front section of belt.

2. Cut two small strips of plain dress fabric 1¼" (3 cm) by 4" (10 cm) and cover ¼" (6 mm) cording to make piping; baste piping to each end of embroidered fabric strip.

3. Cut two strips of plain dress fabric a length equal to one-half of your waist measurement by 4" (10 cm) wide; stitch to each end of piped embroidered strip. The final belt includes 10" (25.5 cm) for overlap in back.

4. Wrap fabric around belting; stitch hook-and-loop tape to overlapped ends in back.

Tips from the designer

■ Think about how much embroidery you want to add, and where. For example, if you want less embellishment, you could embroider only the yoke or the collar and cuffs. If you want more, you could space the rows of embroidery closer together.

■ Make a sampler out of the dress fabric! This is very important, so you can decide how much stabilizer you'll need, which machine needles you'll use, and which decorative stitches will work best.

Plan for the week

Monday:

~~~~~~~

Tuesday:

~~~~~~~

Wednesday:

~~~~~~~

Thursday:

Pretreat fabric; make embroidery samples on fabric swatches.

Friday:

Cut fabric rectangles for bodice pieces; cut out remaining dress pieces, mark, and interface appropriate pieces.

Saturday:

Complete bodice embroidery; cut out bodice and belt pieces; begin dress assembly.

Sunday:

Complete assembly; make buttonholes and sew on buttons; hem; assemble belt.

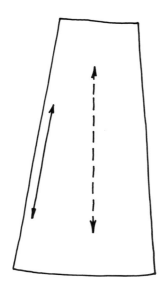

Fig. 1.
Redraw the skirt front and back grainlines down the middle of the pattern, instead of parallel to center front and center back. The finished skirt will hang in a more flattering fashion.

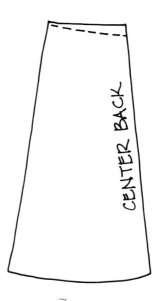

Fig. 2.
Because many women curve in at the back waistline, a skirt can be too long in this area. Lowering the waistline at center back, tapering to zero at the sides, will improve the fit.

Mandarin Red
DESIGNER:
Linda Boyd

Simplicity equals class and elegance in this silk twill coat dress, proving you don't need a lot of details to make a beautiful statement. A few simple changes to the original pattern made this dress especially flattering.

Designer comments

"The short cap sleeves of the original pattern just aren't flattering on anyone older than 30! They also looked tiny, sticking out of the top of a tall column of fabric. It was simple to lengthen the sleeves so they would look in proportion with the rest of the dress and so the upper arms wouldn't be exposed."

Materials and supplies

■ Pattern for single-breasted coat dress

■ Fabric and buttons of choice

Pattern and design changes

1. The designer eliminated the pattern's welt pockets and pocket flaps at the hip, which looked too cluttered on a petite figure, added unneeded width at the hipline, and distorted the sleek line of this straight style.

2. She also added about 3" (7.5 cm) to the sleeve length.

3. She then added walking ease to the front opening, to prevent the dress from spreading open while walking. See Figure 1.

Tips from the designer

■ Sandra Betzina is a serious advocate for walking ease and I agree! Adding walking ease to any front-closing garment is very important if it's not already included in the pattern. The extra ease can be added right at the center front or by slashing and spreading the front pattern piece, and

should be increased the longer the garment is. For example, a knee-length coat dress would benefit from the addition of 1" (2.5 cm) of walking ease at the hem, tapering to zero at the neckline or armhole (whichever is needed for the pattern to remain flat), while an ankle-length overcoat would require 3" (7.5 cm) of walking ease at the hem. The walking ease enables you to move around comfortably in the garment without its spreading open and showing what you're wearing underneath. You won't be able to see the extra fabric in the finished garment, but it makes such a difference!

Plan for the week

Monday:

Tuesday:

Wednesday:

Thursday:

Friday:
Pretreat fabric.

Saturday:
Make pattern alterations and add walking ease to both front pieces; cut out dress, mark, and interface appropriate pieces.

Sunday:
Assemble dress; make buttonholes and sew on buttons; hem.

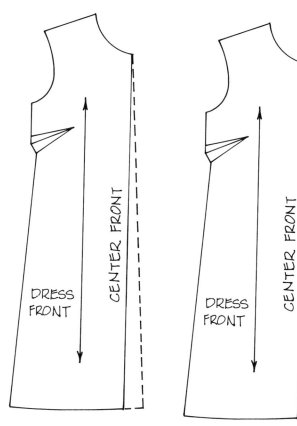

Fig. 1.
Adding walking ease to a front-opening garment will prevent its spreading apart while you walk. Add it at the center front hemline, tapering to zero at the neckline (left), or slash and spread the pattern piece at the hemline, tapering to zero at the neckline or any point that keeps the pattern piece flat (right).

Paisley Panache
DESIGNER:
M. Luanne Carson

The classic coat dress style is comfortable and flattering, but can be a bit conservative. Here, the butter-soft paisley corduroy adds a feminine touch and the contrasting lapel binding creates a distinctive accent—without adding bulk.

Designer comments

"This technique is a melding of binding and appliqué. Contrast fabric is applied to the outer edges of the collar and lapel like a binding, but one of its folded edges happens to be shaped, like an appliqué. It's easy to do, reduces bulk where seams meet, and is a natural for straight-edge closures of blouses, jackets, and wrap skirts, as well as for pocket edges and belts."

Materials and supplies

- Pattern for double-breasted coat dress
- Fabric of choice
- Contrast fabric for appliqué binding
- Fusible interfacing

Pattern and design changes

The designer started with a classic double-breasted coat dress pattern and altered the collar/lapel design to accommodate the decorative contrast binding.

Construction details

1. Eliminate seam allowances on outer edges of upper and under collars, bodice front lapel, and front facing; these edges will be bound by the contrasting fabric.

2. To make a pattern for the binding/appliqué, trace the outer edges of the upper collar and front facing, and shape the inside edges as you wish. Transfer pattern piece grainlines to the binding pattern. See Figure 1.

pieces, wrong side of binding to right side of collar and facing.

7. Sew the upper collar to the front facing at the gorge line.

8. Stitch bodice front to bodice back at shoulders.

9. Sew under collar to bodice neckline.

10. Position the joined collar/facing pieces over the under collar and bodice, wrapping the 1" (2.5 cm) binding seam allowance around the raw edges.

11. Trim away any excess seam allowance and turn under the raw edge of the binding, mitering the points.

12. Sew invisibly by hand to front lapels and under collar.

Tips from the designer

■ When tracing the under collar and front facing to create the pattern for the binding/appliqué, you can shape the inside edges in different designs, for interesting effects. See Figure 3.

Plan for the week

Monday:

Tuesday:

Wednesday:

Thursday:
Pretreat fabric; experiment with different binding edge shapes.

Friday:
Cut out dress, mark, and interface appropriate pieces; cut binding pattern from contrast fabric.

Saturday:
Begin dress assembly; attach contrast binding to upper collar; assemble bound collar.

Sunday:
Complete assembly; make buttonholes and sew on buttons; hem.

3. Add ⅜" (1 cm) seam allowances to the inside edges and 1" (2.5 cm) to the outside edges of the binding (this is the edge that will wrap around the outer edges of the under collar and lapel). See Figure 2.

4. Cut the binding pattern out of contrasting fabric and a fusible interfacing that is compatible with the fabric. Trim seam allowances from interfacing and fuse to fabric, following manufacturer's directions.

5. Press under the ⅜" (1 cm) inside edges of the upper collar and front lapel binding, and place them on the respective garment pieces; evaluate the effect. If you don't like the way it looks, now is the time to redesign a new binding shape.

6. When satisfied with the look, topstitch the shaped edges of the binding pieces to the upper collar and front facing

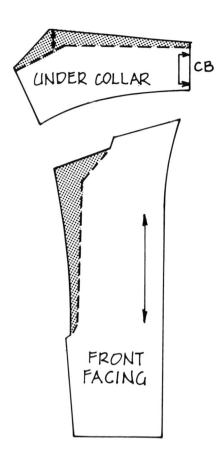

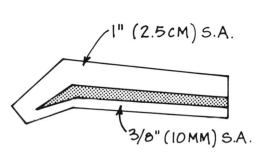

1" (2.5CM) S.A.

3/8" (10MM) S.A.

CB

UNDER COLLAR

FRONT
FACING

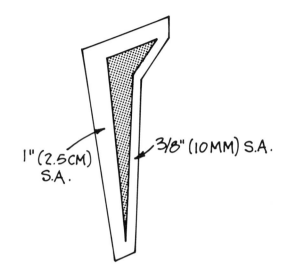

1" (2.5CM)
S.A.

3/8" (10MM) S.A.

Fig. 1.
To make a pattern for the appliqué bind-
ing, trace outside edges of the under col-
lar and facing, shape inside edges as
desired, and mark graintlines.

Fig. 2.
Add 3/8" (1 cm) seam allowance to
inside edges and 1" (2.5 cm) seam
allowance to outside edges of binding
pattern.

FRONT
FACING

UNDER COLLAR

Fig. 3.
Shape the inside edges of the binding for a different effect.

Signature Style
DESIGNER:
Linda Boyd

This classic dress style made out of a crisp linen results in a very professional look. The double-breasted front closure provides a showcase for some unique designer buttons—a simple way to add pizzazz to a conservative style.

Designer comments

"So many dress patterns are too cluttered with design features to look good on short women. This one originally had a big, wide collar, which would look fine on somebody tall but can look like a clown collar on a shorter figure."

Materials and supplies

- Pattern for double-breasted coat dress
- Fabric and buttons of choice

Pattern and design changes

1. The designer cut the collar ¾" (2 cm) narrower all around, to down-scale it for a more petite figure.

2. She also eliminated the pattern's welt pockets and pocket flaps at the hip, which looked too cluttered on a petite figure and added unneeded width at the hipline.

Plan for the week

Monday:

Tuesday:

Wednesday:

Thursday:

Friday:
Pretreat fabric; make pattern alterations.

Saturday:
Cut out dress, mark, and interface appropriate pieces; begin dress assembly.

Sunday:
Complete assembly; make buttonholes and sew on buttons; hem.

Tips from the designer

- Don't be afraid to omit pattern features or alter their scale to look good on you. Pattern companies design their styles for a tall, thin figure with "standard" measurements. Most of us don't match the standard, so patterns need to be customized to our individual needs. Big, bold pattern features may need to be downsized to look in proportion with a smaller figure, while small frills and details may need to be redesigned or scaled up in size for a larger figure.

Animal Kingdom

DESIGNER:
the author

This drop-waist dress illustrates how easy it can be to add some fun to a simple style. Use contrasting colors or prints for the top and bottom. and then accentuate the dividing line with a ruffle of yet another fabric.

Designer comments

"I added the hip ruffle to this straight shift to draw attention away from the waist area and toward the hip area. The result gives a rectangular figure the suggestion of curves."

Materials and supplies

- Pattern for straight drop-waist dress
- Contrasting fabrics of choice
- Fabric for bias-cut ruffle
- Soutache cord for button loops

Pattern and design changes

1. The designer started with a straight drop-waist dress with fully faced bodice. She redrew the front neckline to lower it ½" (1.25 cm), for comfort.

2. She then cut two bias bands, 4" (10 cm) wide by the drop-waist seam length plus 10" (25.5 cm). When sewn together end-to-end for the ruffle, the band had 20" (51 cm) extra for gathering up.

3. She eliminated the full bodice facing and replaced it with armhole and neckline bias bindings made out of the hip ruffle fabric. This resulted in a single layer of fabric in the bodice, for greater comfort under a light jacket or in warm weather.

4. She replaced the back zipper closing with a center back neckline slit and button/loop closure.

Construction details

1. Cut bias strips of self-fabric or contrasting material to face armhole and neckline openings.

2. Assemble bodice; cut cord for button loops and baste at center back neckline seam.

3. Stitch armhole and neckline facings to right side of bodice; turn to inside and topstitch in place.

4. Assemble skirt. To reinforce the top of the slit at the skirt's center back and protect it from ripping when you walk, stitch a bar tack at the top of the slit or appliqué an interesting shape cut from the hip ruffle fabric for design interest. See Figure 1.

5. Assemble hip ruffle and sandwich between bodice and skirt at drop-waist seamline. NOTE: Distribute the gathers of the ruffle unevenly, placing more ruffle at the side seams than at the front or back. This accentuates the flounce at the sides and gives the illusion of curvier hips—good camouflage for someone with a straight up-and-down figure.

Tips from the designer

- The bias bindings for the armhole and neckline could be turned to the outside, as reverse facings, providing another opportunity for creative color blocking or fabric combinations.

- Split the bodice and skirt pattern pieces vertically and color block different fabrics left and right as well as top and bottom. Don't forget to add seam allowances to all split edges.

Plan for the week

Monday:

〜〜〜〜〜

Tuesday:

〜〜〜〜〜

Wednesday:

〜〜〜〜〜

Thursday:

Pretreat fabric; make pattern alterations.

Friday:

Cut out dress, mark, and interface appropriate pieces.

Saturday:

Make hip ruffle; cut armhole and neckline facing strips from
leftover ruffle fabric; begin dress assembly.

Sunday:

Complete assembly; sew on buttons at center
back neckline; hem.

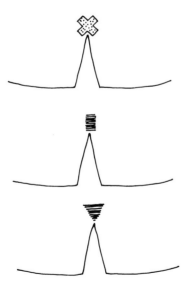

Fig. 1.

*Reinforce the top of a skirt slit so the seam won't rip when you
walk. Use a contrasting fabric appliqué shape (top,) standard
bar tack (center), or shaped bar tack (bottom).*

Purple Pansy Fantasy

DESIGNER:
Sheila Bennitt

With some imagination and luscious fabric, the designer took two simple patterns into new territory—full of dramatic style and flair.

Designer comments

"I like to separate a dress top from the bottom at the waist, hip, or above the knee and then attach a Lycra, tricot, or cotton knit tank top to the skirt. This creates a basic dress that goes with many different tops. The stretchy tank top is comfortable and provides a good base for layering, and then I can get really creative with different versions of the dress top."

Materials and supplies

- Pattern for straight drop-waist dress with flounce
- Pattern for T-shirt tunic
- Fabric of choice and contrast fabric for slip
- Lycra or stretch fabric for dress tank top
- Woolly nylon thread

Tools

- Serger
- Embroidery foot or rolled hem attachment

Pattern and design changes

1. The designer started with a pattern for a straight dress with dropped waist and a short flounced skirt. She replaced the top of the dress with a Lycra tank top and redesigned the flounced bottom of the dress to add inserts for greater volume and a swishy feel.

2. She used a basic T-shirt tunic pattern for the new dress top, adding width at the sleeve ends and a voluminous flounce to the tunic hem, which was then pulled up and anchored at one hip.

3. She then added a draped scarf piece to the dress and anchored it at the shoulders.

Construction details

1. Use a narrow rolled edge finish, stitched with woolly nylon thread, to cleanly finish seam edges and accentuate the frilly, flouncy quality of the fabric.

2. Make the basic flounced skirt again, a bit longer than the dress and cut from contrasting fabric, for a slip to wear underneath.

Tips from the designer

- Think of patterns as nothing more than simple outlines to follow. Then, your mind can take flight and you can inspire yourself to drape the fabric and combine design features in the most interesting ways.

Plan for the week

Monday:

Tuesday:

Wednesday:

Thursday:
Pretreat fabric.

Friday:
Make pattern adjustments for Lycra tank top
and new dress top; cut out dress.

Saturday:
Assemble dress and dress top.

Sunday:
Make draped scarf and slip.

Floral Delights

DESIGNER:
Sheila Bennitt

A drapey fabric like this pretty rayon can be arranged in lots of different ways to enhance any figure and camouflage features you would prefer to forget.

Designer comments

"I love to start from a basic shell and then drape darts, pleats, or tucks that suit my figure. It's a lot like painting. I decide which effects to create as I go."

Materials and supplies

- Pattern for straight drop-waist dress with flounce
- Pattern for T-shirt tunic
- Fabric of choice
- Lycra or stretch fabric for dress tank top
- Woolly nylon thread

Tools

- Serger
- Embroidery foot or rolled hem attachment

Pattern and design changes

1. The designer started with the same basic drop-waist dress pattern as the Purple Pansy Fantasy dress on page 126, with an attached tricot tank top.

2. She also used the same basic T-shirt tunic pattern for the dress top, and then cut two L-shaped pieces for the surplice drapes. See Figure 1.

3. The addition of loops around the neckline hold a self-fabric scarf in place.

Construction details

1. Once the tunic dress top is assembled, stitch one L-shaped piece at the right shoulder and try on. Experiment with different pleats and tucks to create desired shaping, and stitch in place at side seam. See Figure 2.

2. Repeat with other L-shaped piece for left side.

3. Gather and roll-hem a scrap of fabric for the flower trim at the skirt flounce.

Tips from the designer

- Play around with different pleat and tuck arrangements until you get the draped effect you want. Just remember that until you stitch everything in place, you're free to experiment. Only you will know the intermediate steps you went through to arrive at the beautiful result.

Plan for the week

Monday:

Tuesday:

Wednesday:

Thursday:

Friday:
Pretreat fabric; make adjustments for dress tank top and tunic top.

Saturday:
Cut out dress, surplice top, and surplice drapes; begin assembly.

Sunday:
Finish assembly; attach surplice drapes and flower trim.

Fig. 1.
The surplice drapes are simply made from two L-shaped pieces of self-fabric. The raw edges are roll-hemmed for a ripply effect.

Fig. 2.
The drapes are attached at the shoulders, tucked for the desired effect, and then attached at the sides.

129

A Sweetheart Affair

DESIGNER:

Sally Hickerson

It can be so simple to combine favorite patterns, make a few alterations, and end up with a great-looking, original style. The dress shown here is put together from the designer's favorite blouse and skirt patterns.

Materials and supplies

- Pattern for scoop-neck blouse with buttoned front opening
- Pattern for full gathered skirt
- Fabric of choice
- Elastic for waistline casing

Pattern and design changes

1. The designer started with a scoop-neck blouse pattern. She redrew the front neckline in a sweetheart shape, starting from the shoulder seams. Because the newly drawn edges are slightly curved or bowed toward the center, the neckline does not gap open. See Figure 1.

2. She chose a favorite skirt pattern, added side seam pockets, and put it together with the blouse pattern to make the dress.

Construction details

1. When combining the blouse and skirt patterns to make a dress, shorten the blouse pattern pieces to about 1" (2.5 cm) below the waistline mark. Note that you might not need to make the bottom buttonhole.

2. Take up the waistline ease of the skirt by making an elastic casing at the blouse/skirt seamline, to create a breezy, blousy, comfortable dress.

Designer comments

"I didn't like the wide-open scoop neck of the original blouse pattern, so I just kept drawing neckline shapes on pattern-drafting paper until I came up with one I liked. Then, I pulled out my favorite skirt pattern, made a few changes, and attached it to the blouse."

Tips from the designer

- To keep the neckline from gapping open, shape the new curves in toward the body and keep the shoulder seams and center back where they are—don't lower them or spread them out. You won't have to worry about making the neck opening large enough to fit over your head if you have a buttoned front opening—another safeguard against gapping.

■ When combining patterns, think about fabrics that will be appropriate for the finished garment, not the components. For example, the fabric I chose for this dress needed to be drapey enough to look good gathered at the waistline; it would not have worked as well for the original skirt pattern.

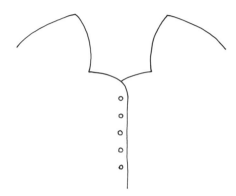

Fig. 1.
It's easy to change a scoop-neck blouse to a sweetheart style. If the front neckline edges are curved slightly toward the center, they won't gap open.

Plan for the week

Monday:

~~~~~~~~~

Tuesday:

~~~~~~~~~

Wednesday:

~~~~~~~~~

Thursday:
Pretreat fabric.

Friday:
Draw new neckline; cut out blouse and skirt, mark, and interface appropriate pieces.

Saturday:
Assemble blouse; make buttonholes and sew on buttons.

Sunday:
Make and attach skirt to blouse; hem.

A Gardener's Jumper

DESIGNER:
Karen Swing

This dress-weight denim jumper combines the flattering fit of princess seams with the comfort and ease of a wrap-front opening. The free-form appliqué adds a beautiful, one-of-a-kind effect, while the coordinated bias binding and covered buttons are the perfect finishing touch.

Designer comments

"The print fabric appliqué and free-form embroidery provide an opportunity for you to put your artistic eye to work— arranging design motifs and stitching them down the way you like them."

Materials and supplies

- Wrap-front jumper pattern

- Fabric of choice, plus ½ yard (.5 m) for bias binding

- ½ yard (.5 m) cotton fabric with large design motifs, for appliqué, bias binding, button loops, and covered buttons

- Several large spools of thread to complement or match print fabric

- Spray starch

- Covered button kit

Pattern and design changes

The designer replaced the armhole and front opening/neckline facing with self-fabric bias binding and print fabric bias binding, to provide a nice edging for the appliqué. She also used print fabric binding to create complementary button loops.

Construction details

For the appliqué:

1. When cutting out the front pattern piece, add an extra ½" (1.25 cm) or so to the front opening edge; you will trim this off after embroidery. Once pattern pieces are cut out, stay stitch or serge all edges to prevent stretching while working with them.

2. Do not cut out neck, armhole, or front edge facings. Instead, reserve an end of the yardage to make bias binding.

3. To stabilize the fabric for machine embroidery, spray starch generously on right side of right front piece; let dry, then flip over and spray the wrong side. Let dry thoroughly.

4. Cut out the printed fabric to match the front opening edge of the jumper, reserving an end of the yardage for the bias binding.

5. Using your artistic eye, cut around the fabric's design motifs to create an interesting inside edge. The appliqué doesn't have to be in one piece; you can cut out separate design elements (individual leaves, flowers, etc.) and place them where you want them.

6. Pin the printed fabric appliqué and individual elements to the jumper front. To begin the embroidery, choose a thread color to match the jumper fabric or the main color of the printed fabric, and free-form stitch the appliqué to the entire front with a long machine stitch. Take care to keep the stitching from puckering the fabric.

7. Cover the entire appliqué evenly with embroidery, one color at a time. Vary the thread colors as you wish, remembering that shiny threads will appear to come forward and matte-finish threads will recede. Stitch off the printed fabric onto the jumper fabric, to add interest and visually soften the edge between the two fabrics. Each time you change thread colors, steam the jumper front well on both sides to maintain the shape.

8. When stitching along a raw edge, decrease the stitch length to seal the edge. Vary stitch lengths for interest. Keep

stitching until you like the look.

9. When finished, steam and press the jumper front well. Lay out the pattern piece on the jumper front, aligning all edges except front opening; trim excess fabric along front opening.

For bias binding:

1. Create and pin button loops to right side of right front, and baste securely in place. Looped ends should point to inside of garment; raw ends should line up with raw edge of jumper front.

2. Create bias binding out of the jumper fabric and the printed fabric, and then stitch it to the front edge, changing from one to the other to match the change from appliqué to jumper fabric. About 4" (10 cm) from the point where you will switch from one to the other, backstitch and cut threads. Then stitch ends of two different bias pieces together; press seam open; and continue to stitch to front edge.

3. Bind armholes with jumper fabric, starting a little beyond the underarm seam to prevent added bulk.

4. Turn all bias binding to inside and blind stitch to wrong side of fabric.

5. Whipstitch button loops to bound front edge so they will lie flat.

Tips from the designer

■ The spray starch is a great stabilizer. You can use your outstretched hands to hold the fabric securely as you free-form embroider, but you may be more comfortable using an embroidery hoop.

■ When stitching the bias bindings to the front and back neckline and the bottom half of the armholes, pull the bias slightly. This will prevent the dreaded "gaposis," or gapping. Conversely, do not pull the binding too tightly when stitching the front, so it will hang straight and not curl.

■ When covering the buttons with the printed fabric, cut an extra circle of thin white fabric, such as muslin, for a lining. The two layers of fabric will keep the metal from showing through.

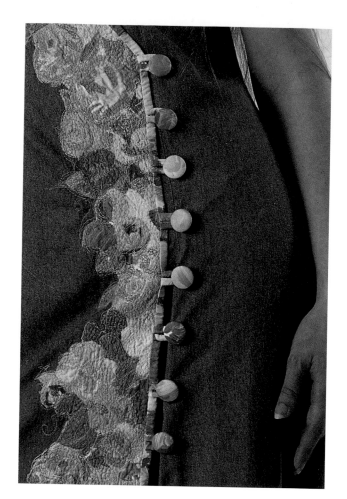

Plan for the week

Monday:

Tuesday:

Wednesday:

Thursday:
Pretreat fabric.

Friday:
Cut out jumper, mark; stabilize fabric for embroidery.

Saturday:
Cut appliqué designs and stitch to jumper front; begin jumper assembly.

Sunday:
Complete assembly; make button loops and bias binding, and attach to jumper front; cover and sew on buttons; hem.

Travel in Style

DESIGNER:
Sheila Bennitt

For versatility, nothing works better than designing a wardrobe of dress tops to go with a basic dress bottom. This outfit is great for traveling because it's made out of easy-care cotton knit, and it can be layered in a number of ways for different occasions.

Designer comments

"Each piece in this collection has a different design accent, and they all can be made in under an hour or just a little bit more."

Materials and supplies

- Pattern for straight or empire waist dress with front slit
- Pattern for T-shirt tunic
- Fabric of choice
- Lycra or stretch fabric for dress tank top
- Printed cottons for appliqués
- Ribbed knit edging
- Decorative buttons

Pattern and design changes

1. The designer started with a simple empire waist dress with front skirt slit. She cut the dress skirt section off and added a tricot tank top.

2. She used the same basic T-shirt tunic pattern as in the Purple Pansy Fantasy dress on page 126 for a basic dress top, along with a matching knotted self-fabric necktie.

3. She then created two more dress tops from the same T-shirt pattern. One features shortened sleeves, ribbed knit edging, a printed cotton appliqué, and decorative button trim. The other is made from a striped denim with decorative floral appliqué.

4. To demonstrate the versatility of her collection, the designer made a fourth coordinating dress top with asymmetrical

hemline from the fabric left over from a skirt flounce (see designer tip below). It can be made with straight sleeves, cuffed sleeves, or drawn to the inside for a puffed look. This outfit is accessorized with a hand-painted self-fabric scarf with button trim.

Tips from the designer

■ If you make a skirt flounce like the one in the Purple Pansy Fantasy or Floral Delights dress from a very wide fabric, you can cut the circular flounce in one piece (without seams) by double-folding the fabric. See Figure 1. The funny curved pieces that are left over (as shown in Figure 2) become the basis for the fourth coordinating dress top above—all I had to do was cut them to size, create the neckline, and add sleeves. Easy, fun, and no-waste!

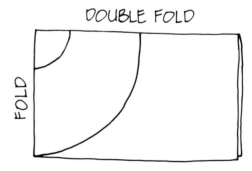

Fig. 1.
A skirt flounce can be cut in one piece out of wide fabric folded twice.

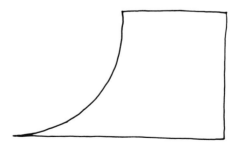

Fig. 2.
The odd-shaped pieces of fabric left over from cutting the skirt flounce can be used as the front and back pieces of a tunic top with asymmetrical hem.

Plan for the week

Monday:

Tuesday:

Wednesday:

Thursday:
Pretreat fabric; make pattern adjustments for dress tank top and coordinating T-shirt tunics.

Friday:
Cut out dress and tunic tops.

Saturday:
Assemble dress and two tunic tops.

Sunday:
Make appliqués and assemble two tunic tops; make scarf and knotted self-fabric necktie.

Joyce Baldwin

is Assistant Professor of Textiles at Western Carolina University in Cullowhee, North Carolina. She passes on her love of fabrics and fashion design to classrooms full of students, and plans annual student trips to the New York City fashion centers, where she also manages to shop for sewing supplies for her own studio.

Karen M. Bennett

of Alexander, North Carolina, has been a member of the Southern Highland Handicraft Guild since 1983. An energetic woman, she home schools her four children, keeps a large organic garden, sells her tatting, embroidery, and sewing in galleries and shops, and teaches classes for the local chapter of the Embroiderer's Guild of America. A career highlight was the 1993 commission of a tatted angel for the White House Christmas tree.

Sheila Bennitt

recently relocated to Asheville, North Carolina from Texas, where she sold fanciful fashions from her design studio. She is also a painter and sees many parallels in design and technique between working with fabric and paint.

Linda Boyd

is a walking encyclopedia of sewing expertise and has been a professional dressmaker for many years. She now reserves her sewing time, which she calls her "fun time," for herself and her family. Linda lives in Leicester, North Carolina.

M. Luanne Carson

thrives on the creative process of integrating fabric and style for unusual effect. She combines her formal training in clothing and textiles with her success as an educator to excite her students about their creative potential. Even after 40 years at the machine, sewing continues to galvanize Luanne's thoughts and activities.

Sally Hickerson

is the hospitable owner of Waechter's Silk Shop in Asheville, North Carolina, a favorite destination for fabric lovers. She also is an expert manager of her time, because she gets a lot of sewing done. Sally is a specialist in customizing patterns for her petite figure and adding flair to everything she makes.

Lisa Mandle

is the owner and principal designer of Only One, a custom one-of-a-kind clothing and accessories business in Marshall, North Carolina. She has had extensive experience in the fashion and costume design fields, and was selected in 1984 as one of the top ten designers in Washington, D.C. In her current business, she emphasizes the unique qualities of clothing and never makes a design from the collection the same way twice—hence the name, Only One.

Marion E. Mathews

of Asheville, North Carolina, got hooked on sewing when her grandmother let her use the old treadle machine. Since then, she has made her own wedding dress, children's clothes, men's sport coats, and much more. Although Marion soon switched from the treadle machine to a motorized version, she, too, passed on her love of sewing and fabric—to her daughter, the author.

Tracy Munn

is a sewing dynamo who recently built a separate barn/studio to house her many fabrics and supplies. She had a dressmaking business in South Carolina, before moving to Asheville, North Carolina in 1995. She loves making clothes for her family and home decorating items for her bungalow in the country.

Carolyn Nordgren

turned her sewing hobby into a business six years ago and now sells her appliquéd women's apparel at craft shows around the Southeast. Her first venture, sewing dolls, did not succeed, so she switched to making clothing. She lives in Hendersonville, North Carolina.

Mary S. Parker

is descended from a long line of quilters and seamstresses. Her love of sewing and a fondness for cats have remained constant throughout a changing array of professional career positions. Mary lives in Asheville, North Carolina, and recently moved into a larger house with her understanding husband so that she would have sufficient room for her growing fabric stash.

Joneen M. Sargent

likes the creative outlet that sewing provides and loves to try new things. She started sewing back in high school and makes quilts and clothing for herself and her family. Joneen lives in Bristol, Tennessee.

Elizabeth Searle

started sewing in the crib, according to her grandmother. She has a dressmaking business in Asheville, North Carolina, teaches creative sewing techniques in area classes, and still has time to experiment with creative art-to-wear clothing for herself and her clients.

Sherida Ann Stone

says she has been sewing "forever," at least since she was in an 8th grade Home Economics class. She proceeded to get a Bachelor of Fine Arts degree at Syracuse University in New York and now combines her design education with her love of nice fabrics. She lives in Weaverville, North Carolina.

Karen Swing

has been sewing since she was 12 years old and is now a full-time fabric artist in Boone, North Carolina. She makes art quilts, but her first love is one-of-a-kind wearables. Karen has particularly been enjoying machine embroidery and experimenting with the effects of dyeing different fabrics and materials.

A book is a lot like a custom garment, needing various underpinnings and support systems that may be invisible to the casual observer, yet are absolutely necessary for the quality and look of the finished product. Sincere thanks are due to these behind-the-scenes folks, for their talents and their generosity.

Heartfelt thanks go to all the designers, whose impressive creativity and passion for sewing gave this book a reason to be. Their enthusiasm was so contagious that I was inspired to get quite a bit of sewing done myself while working on this book.

Special thanks are due to everyone involved with the photography:

■ Richard Babb, whose view through the camera you see on these pages.

■ the professionals at Weststar Photographic, who processed the film immediately, so we could quickly get a feel for the book.

■ the folks at Stuf Antiques and Magnolia Beauregard's, who generously lent some of their treasures for photo props.

■ the models, who good-naturedly and beautifully brought the dresses to life—Evans Carter, Jessi Cinque, Celia Naranjo, Joanne Badr, Mara Dennis, Betty Clark, Brigid Burns, Sharon Ray, Christina Faulk, Beth Benischek, Deborah Swider, M. Luanne Carson, and Amy Sue Ball.

Thank you to Tracy Munn, who made two emergency trips to the sewing shop to replace missing buttons on one of the dresses. To Mary Morris for the tour of G Street Fabrics' equipment and supply departments. And to Sally Hickerson, who generously allowed us to use her store, Waechter's Silk Shop, as a pick-up and drop-off point for the dresses. Finally, thank you to Bob Bowles, my husband, for his gentle support and uncomplaining patience with dresses hanging all over the house.

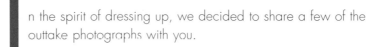

n the spirit of dressing up, we decided to share a few of the outtake photographs with you.

143